The Best of Rose Elliot

The Ultimate Vegetarian Collection

The Best of Rose Elliot

The Ultimate Vegetarian Collection

150 DELICIOUS RECIPES

hamlyn

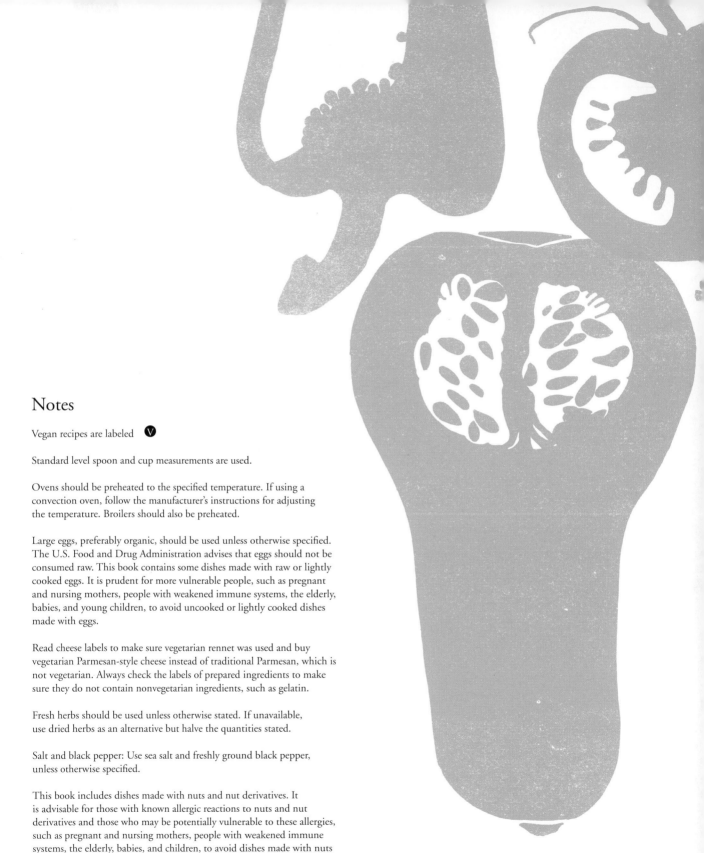

Notes

Vegan recipes are labeled **Ⓥ**

Standard level spoon and cup measurements are used.

Ovens should be preheated to the specified temperature. If using a convection oven, follow the manufacturer's instructions for adjusting the temperature. Broilers should also be preheated.

Large eggs, preferably organic, should be used unless otherwise specified. The U.S. Food and Drug Administration advises that eggs should not be consumed raw. This book contains some dishes made with raw or lightly cooked eggs. It is prudent for more vulnerable people, such as pregnant and nursing mothers, people with weakened immune systems, the elderly, babies, and young children, to avoid uncooked or lightly cooked dishes made with eggs.

Read cheese labels to make sure vegetarian rennet was used and buy vegetarian Parmesan-style cheese instead of traditional Parmesan, which is not vegetarian. Always check the labels of prepared ingredients to make sure they do not contain nonvegetarian ingredients, such as gelatin.

Fresh herbs should be used unless otherwise stated. If unavailable, use dried herbs as an alternative but halve the quantities stated.

Salt and black pepper: Use sea salt and freshly ground black pepper, unless otherwise specified.

This book includes dishes made with nuts and nut derivatives. It is advisable for those with known allergic reactions to nuts and nut derivatives and those who may be potentially vulnerable to these allergies, such as pregnant and nursing mothers, people with weakened immune systems, the elderly, babies, and children, to avoid dishes made with nuts and nut oils. It is also prudent to check the labels of prepared ingredients for the possible inclusion of nut derivatives.

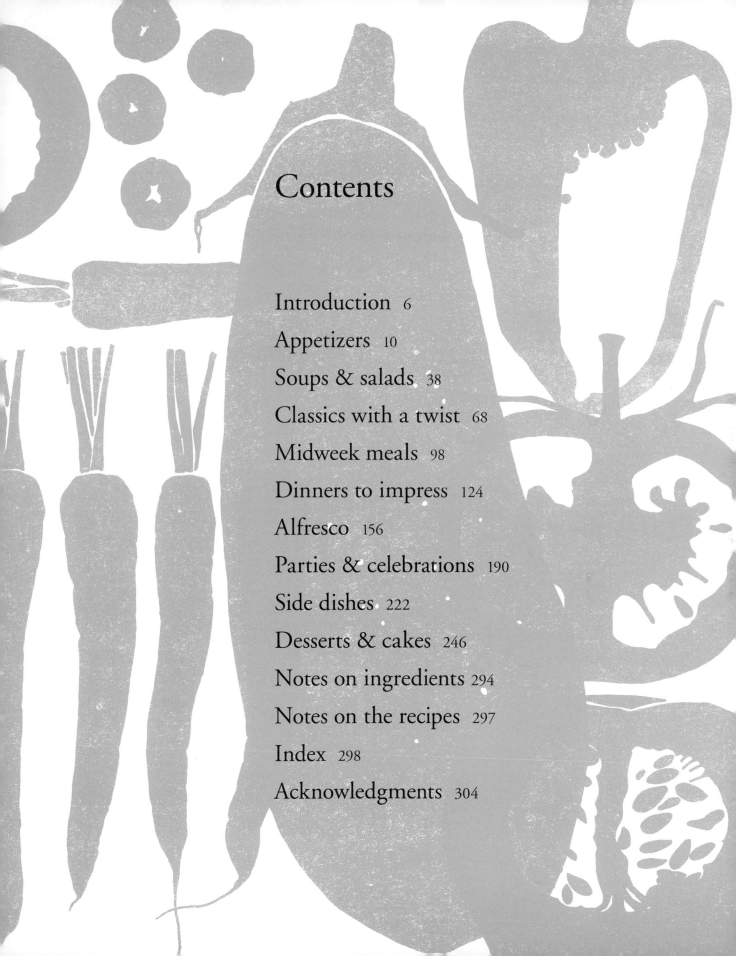

Contents

Introduction

Welcome to my new vegetarian collection. It's such a pleasure to see the recipes from *Vegetarian Supercook* and *Veggie Chic* brought together in one book, and I think you'll agree that it's a real feast. I loved writing those two books, and looking through this new collection brings back so many memories. It is always fun trying out new ideas and getting the reaction of others—my husband, my daughters, my grandchildren, whoever is around—and I can rely on them all for frank comments and often helpful suggestions. One such time was when I was experimenting with the recipe for Wild Mushroom Tempura. One of my daughters came in with several friends, so what began as a quiet evening recipe-testing "home alone" turned into a memorable kitchen party, and one of my happiest-ever tasting sessions, full of laughter and fun. You can see the results on page 29.

But first, let me give you an idea of what else is in store in this beautiful book. Divided into nine chapters, roughly arranged in meal order, it begins with appetizers and ends with desserts and cakes, with meals for every occasion in between.

The Appetizers chapter begins with one of my most popular recipes: Goat Cheese & Cranberry Packages. Everyone loves this because it's so pretty, and also—like the majority of the recipes in this book—so easy to make. And I must mention the Rosemary Sorbet, which is such a refreshing (and also boozy) palate cleanser between courses.

In Classics with a Twist, you'll find variations on conventional dishes. Veggie versions of meat dishes, such as Lentil Casserole with Mashed Potatoes; funky updates of vegetarian classics, such as Thai-Flavored Mushroom Stroganoff with Golden Rice; and some delectable lower carb versions of favorite recipes, such as No-Rice Nori Sushi, Omelet Cannelloni with Spinach Filling and Tagliatelle of Cabbage with Cream Cheese, Herb & Garlic Sauce.

Although most of the recipes in this book are fairly quick to make (some especially so), the chapter to turn to, when you're short of time and want something fast and tasty, is Midweek Meals. These include speedy, not snacky, dishes that you could eat straight from the pan, such as Corn Fritters with Tomato Sauce or Rosti with Applesauce (so yummy).

I was writing *Veggie Chic* when my youngest daughter got married, and for the reception, the caterer used the recipes that I was creating for the book. I still can't make any of them without being transported back to the hottest day of that year and one of the happiest days of my life. It was many people's first experience of a fully vegetarian wedding and I was told we made one or two converts that day. The caterer later told me he was continuing to use the recipes, which had become part of his repertoire.

Vegetarians often miss out at parties and receptions, so having some recipes for vegetarian canapés is particularly useful. The Baby Popovers with Nut Roast & Horseradish are always a sensation, as are the Mini Carrot & Cardamom Tarte Tatins—and there are plenty of others: vegetarian (or vegan) guests need never be neglected if you have this book.

Of course, there are some show-stopping main courses and desserts, too. Both the Wild Mushroom Roulade and Moroccan-Flavored Eggplant Wellington spring to mind as examples of the former, while as a final flourish the Dreamy Raspberry & Rose Meringue and Berry Skewers with White Chocolate Dip always evoke gasps of delight and appreciation.

The Lemon & Almond Drizzle Cake—so simple, so fast to make, so loved by everyone who tries it—seems to have become one of the "signature dishes" of *Veggie Chic*, just as Whiskey Cream Banana Pie has with *Vegetarian Supercook*. You've just got to try them! If you want to know some of my personal favorites, I love the Little Lemon Cheesecakes with Blueberries because they're so quick to make, look so pretty, and can easily be made vegan, too; and I love the Chili Kulfi, which also work really well when made with the pouring vegan soy cream.

Coming back down to earth, literally as well as figuratively, I love eating outside and you'll find me there at the first hint of sunshine, probably enjoying something from the Alfresco chapter of this book. If you're looking for something different for a veggie barbecue, try Dough Ball, Haloumi & Olive Skewers or Baby Potatoes & Mushrooms on Rosemary Skewers.

It's often the little touches that make a meal memorable and special. I often include a great accompaniment as part of a recipe, but side dishes also have a chapter to themselves. These complement and enhance the dishes and many of them can also stand alone as appetizers, snacks, or light main dishes. Who could resist Roasted Potatoes in Sea Salt & Balsamic Vinegar? Or Parsnips in Sage Butter?

In fact, I'm really encouraging you to try everything that appeals to you. If there's one thing I'd like to give you, through this book, it's confidence in yourself and your ability to make beautiful, tasty food. This—confidence—is what I find so many people lack. The answer, as with so many things, is practice! The more you cook, the more confident you become, and the more confident you become, the more you want to cook … you get quicker at doing the processes, and bolder with the flavorings. Remember to taste as you work—please use clean teaspoons and don't "double dip"—and make sure to add enough seasoning; I find that many people err on the side of caution and tend to under season food.

But having said that, whatever the cooking writer might say, the important thing is to make the food taste good to you! I recommend you read a recipe all the way through before starting, and if you can, visualize yourself doing each process. And even if things take an unexpected turn, such as a roulade splitting as you roll it up, or a soufflé sinking a little, who's going to complain? Garnish it prettily and present it with a flourish!

I do hope you will enjoy using this book. It really does come with my love! You are in my mind as I create, taste, and write the recipes, and I hope you will like making them as much as I do. Enjoy the process; choose recipes that really appeal to you and make you feel upbeat and happy; change some of the ingredients or flavorings to suit you—have fun. I wish you happiness, confidence, and many wonderful veggie meals.

Rose Elliot

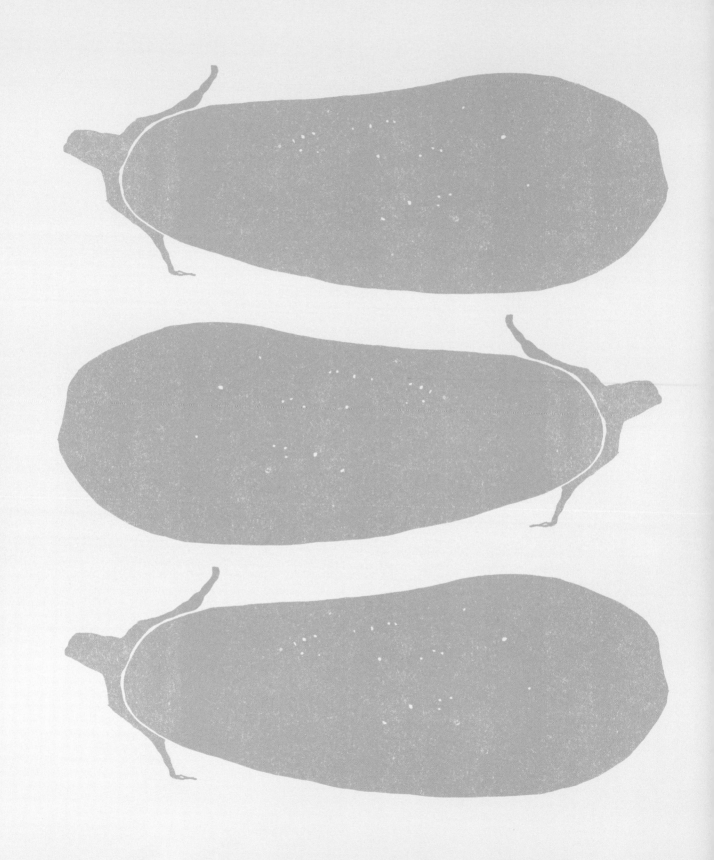

Appetizers

Goat cheese & cranberry packages

SERVES 4
PREPARATION 15 MINUTES
COOKING 15–20 MINUTES

4 sheets of phyllo pastry, 16 x 9 inches
2 (4 oz) goat cheese logs
3–4 tablespoons olive oil, plus extra
   for greasing
4 heaping teaspoons cranberry sauce
leafy salad and vinaigrette dressing
   (see page 66), to serve

1 Cut each piece of phyllo into 4 quarters. Cut the cheeses in half widthwise.

2 To make a package, put one of the pieces of phyllo on a work surface and brush with olive oil. Put another piece over it at right angles to make a cross and brush with olive oil again. Lay a third piece diagonally, as if you were making a star shape, brush with oil, then top with the final piece, diagonally, to complete the "star," and brush with oil.

3 Place one of the pieces of cheese, cut side up, in the center of the pastry and put a heaping teaspoon of cranberry sauce on top of it. Fold up the sides of the phyllo and scrunch them at the top so they hold together. Brush all over with olive oil. Make 3 more packages in the same way.

4 Place all the packages on a lightly oiled baking sheet and bake in a preheated oven, at 400°F, for 15–20 minutes, or until crisp and lightly browned. Serve immediately with a leafy salad dressed with vinaigrette—I think an endive and watercress salad goes well because the bitterness contrasts with the sweet cranberry sauce. Alternatively, if you have the time to make them, some creamy mashed potatoes and fine green beans go well with the packages.

Hot hazelnut-coated Vignotte
with red currant relish

SERVES 4
PREPARATION 10 MINUTES
COOKING 5 MINUTES

10 oz Vignotte cheese or mild goat
   cheese
1 cup chopped skinned hazelnuts
1 egg, beaten
salad greens and vinaigrette dressing
   (see page 66), to serve

FOR THE RED CURRANT RELISH

1 cup red currants or cranberries
   (to make a cranberry relish if you
   can't find red currants)
1 tablespoon sugar (or ⅓ cup if using
   cranberries
squeeze of lemon juice (or orange juice
   if using cranberries)

1 Remove any labels stuck on the cheese, then cut it widthwise into 8 pieces, retaining the rind. Spread the hazelnuts out on a plate.

2 Dip the pieces of cheese first into the beaten egg, then into the hazelnuts, making sure that all surfaces are thickly coated. Put the pieces of coated cheese onto a sheet of nonstick parchment paper and chill until required.

3 To make the red currant relish, put the red currants with the sugar and lemon juice into a saucepan. Bring to a boil, then remove from the heat and set aside. Alternatively, make a cranberry relish by heating the sugar with ⅓ cup of water in a saucepan until the sugar dissolves, then adding the cranberries. Bring to a boil, add a squeeze of orange, then let simmer for about 10 minutes, until the cranberries burst and are tender.

4 Just before you want to serve the meal, transfer the cheese to a baking sheet and cook, rind side down, under a preheated hot broiler for about 5 minutes, or until the nuts are crisp and golden brown. Gently reheat the red currant (or cranberry) relish.

5 While the cheese is cooking, line 4 plates with a few salad greens and drizzle them with a little of the vinaigrette.

6 Serve the sizzling pieces of cheese on top of the leaves, with some of the red currant (or cranberry) relish spooned on top and the rest in a small bowl.

Tomato & Parmesan tarts
with basil cream

SERVES 4

PREPARATION 15 MINUTES,
   PLUS STANDING FOR THE
   BASIL CREAM, IF POSSIBLE

COOKING 35 MINUTES

12 oz frozen ready-to-bake all-butter
   puff pastry (see page 295)
½ cup grated Parmesan-style cheese
3 cups halved cherry tomatoes
2 teaspoons sugar
salt and black pepper

FOR THE BASIL CREAM

bunch of basil, stems removed,
   leaves lightly chopped
⅓ cup light cream or
   olive oil

1 To make the basil cream, mix the basil with the cream or olive oil, season
   with a little salt and black pepper, and let stand—this gets better and
   better as it stands, so it can be made hours in advance, if convenient.

2 Spread the pastry out on a board and cut 4 circles to fit into 4 inch
   shallow, round loose-bottom tart pans.

3 Put the pastry into the tart pans and trim the edges as necessary. Prick
   the pastry all over with a fork. Bake in a preheated oven, at 400°F, for
   15 minutes, until golden brown—the pastry will puff up, so press it
   down gently with the back of a spoon. Remove the tart shells from
   the oven.

4 Sprinkle the Parmesan over the top of the tart shells—this keeps the
   pastry dry and crisp. Toss the tomatoes with the sugar and some salt
   and black pepper and divide them among the tart shells—fill them
   generously because the tomatoes will shrink a little as they cook.

5 Put the tarts back into the oven and bake for 20 minutes. Remove the
   tarts from their pans, place on warmed plates, and swirl some of the basil
   cream over the top of each one. Serve at once.

Bloody Mary gelatins

These gelatins are best made not too far in advance and kept in a cool place instead of in the refrigerator. This recipe can be vegan if you use nondairy horseradish sauce and soy cream from a health-food store.

SERVES 4
PREPARATION 15 MINUTES,
   PLUS SETTING
COOKING 2 MINUTES

1¾ cups tomato juice
1 teaspoon agar powder
   (see page 294)
1½ tablespoons lemon juice
⅓ cup vodka
2 teaspoons vegetarian Worcestershire
   sauce (see page 296)
½ teaspoon Tabasco sauce
2 tablespoons each finely chopped
   red onion, celery, and green bell
   pepper, plus a little more chopped
   red onion and celery, to garnish
1 tablespoon horseradish sauce
3 tablespoons light cream
salt and black pepper

1 Put the tomato juice into a saucepan, gradually sprinkle the agar powder over the cold juice, and stir until it has dissolved. Slowly bring to a boil, then remove from the heat immediately and stir in the lemon juice, vodka, Worcestershire sauce, Tabasco, and some salt and black pepper.

2 Divide the chopped vegetables among 4 small bowls or glasses. Pour the tomato gelatin on top and let set for at least 30 minutes. Cool until required but don't refrigerate.

3 To serve, mix the horseradish sauce with the cream and swirl some over the top of each gelatin. Sprinkle a little chopped red onion and celery over each one to garnish.

Rosemary sorbet ⓥ

Serve as a light appetizer or as a palate refresher between courses. Be warned—it's quite alcoholic.

SERVES 4
PREPARATION 15 MINUTES,
    PLUS COOLING AND FREEZING
COOKING 2 MINUTES

2 cups water
¾ cup granulated sugar
5 rosemary sprigs
1 cup white wine
¼ cup lemon juice
a few small sprigs and flowers of
    rosemary, to decorate (optional)

1 Put the water and sugar into a saucepan with 4 of the rosemary sprigs and bring to a boil. Remove from the heat, cover, and let cool, allowing for the flavor of the rosemary to steep.

2 Remove the rosemary from the cooled syrup and stir in the wine and lemon juice. Chop the remaining sprig of rosemary and stir in.

3 Pour the mixture into a shallow container and freeze for about 2 hours, or until firm, scraping down the sides and beating as it solidifies. Alternatively, freeze in an ice cream maker until the mixture is soft and slushy, then transfer to a plastic container and freeze until required.

4 Remove the sorbet from the freezer about 15 minutes before you want to serve it, then scoop it into bowls and decorate with rosemary sprigs and flowers, if desired.

Eggplant & mozzarella scallops

The morsels of mozzarella wrapped in thin eggplant slices, crumbed, and deep-fried make a tasty appetizer, served with tomato sauce.

SERVES 4
PREPARATION 20 MINUTES
COOKING 30 MINUTES

1 fat eggplant, stem trimmed
olive oil, for brushing
3 oz mozzarella cheese
1 egg, beaten
dried bread crumbs, for coating
canola oil or peanut oil, for
    deep-frying
salt and black pepper

FOR THE TOMATO SAUCE

1 tablespoon olive oil
1 onion, chopped
2 garlic cloves, finely chopped
1 (14½ oz) can diced tomatoes

1 First make the tomato sauce. Heat the olive oil in a saucepan, add the onion, cover, and cook for about 8 minutes, until almost tender. Add the garlic and cook for another 2 minutes, then stir in the tomatoes and cook, uncovered, for about 20 minutes, or until thick. Puree in a food processor or blender, then season and set aside.

2 Meanwhile, for the scallops, cut 20 disks from the eggplant, making them as thin as you can—about ⅛ inch if possible. Brush them on both sides with olive oil and cook under a preheated hot broiler for about 5 minutes, or until tender but not browned. Season them with salt and black pepper.

3 Cut the mozzarella into 20 cubes, put one cube in the center of an eggplant disk, and fold the eggplant over like a mini calzone to make a "scallop." Dip in beaten egg, then dried bread crumbs. Repeat with the remaining eggplant. Put the coated eggplant scallops on a piece of nonstick parchment paper and chill until required.

4 Heat the canola oil or peanut oil in a wok to 350–375°F, or until a cube of bread browns in 30 seconds. Add the eggplant scallops and deep-fry until crisp and golden all over, turning them as necessary. Drain on paper towels.

5 Serve 5 on each plate, with the tomato sauce drizzled around the edge.

Spinach custards with avocado

SERVES 4
PREPARATION 20 MINUTES
COOKING 35–40 MINUTES

butter, for greasing
7½ cups spinach
1¼ cups heavy cream
2 eggs
grated nutmeg
1 large ripe avocado
salt and black pepper

FOR THE LEMON VINAIGRETTE

3 tablespoons lemon juice
½ cup plus 1 tablespoon olive oil

1 Grease four ½–⅔ cup ramekins or other suitable heatproof molds with butter and line the bottoms with circles of nonstick parchment paper.

2 Wash the spinach, then place in a saucepan with just the water clinging to the leaves and cook for about 6 minutes, or until tender. Drain well in a colander, squeezing out as much water as possible, then chop.

3 Put the spinach into a food processor with the cream and eggs and blend to a puree, then season with grated nutmeg, salt, and black pepper.

4 Pour the mixture into the prepared molds, then stand them in a roasting pan and pour in boiling water around them to come halfway up the sides of the molds. Bake in a preheated oven, at 350°F, for 30 minutes, or until firm on top and a toothpick inserted into the center comes out clean. Remove from the oven and let cool.

5 To make the vinaigrette, whisk the lemon juice with the olive oil and some salt and black pepper.

6 Slip a knife around the edges of the molds to loosen, then turn them out onto individual plates. Peel and slice the avocado and arrange some slices on each plate. Season with salt and black pepper, then spoon the lemon vinaigrette over the avocado and the custards and serve warm or cold.

Vietnamese spring rolls ⓥ

These unusual spring rolls are made from rice pancakes and are served uncooked, with a spicy dipping sauce. They taste very fresh and delicious; serve as an appetizer or snack, or with Sesame-roasted Tofu (see page 114) and rice.

SERVES 4
PREPARATION 30 MINUTES

2 oz thin rice noodles
   (one bundle from a package)
1½ cups bean sprouts
1 red bell pepper, cored, seeded,
   and finely sliced
2 teaspoons chopped mint
2 teaspoons chopped cilantro
3 scallions, finely chopped
3 tablespoons teriyaki sauce
8 rice flour pancakes

FOR THE PEANUT DIP

2 tablespoons chunky peanut butter
2 teaspoons packed brown sugar
½ inch piece of fresh ginger root,
   grated
1 garlic clove, crushed
¼ teaspoon dried red pepper flakes
⅓–½ cup soy sauce

1 Put the noodles into a bowl, cover with boiling water, and let soak for 5 minutes, or prepare according to the package directions, until tender, then drain well and place in a bowl.

2 Add the bean sprouts, red bell pepper, mint, cilantro, scallions, and teriyaki sauce and mix well, making sure the ingredients are well distributed.

3 Spread a clean, damp dish towel over the work surface. Put the rice pancakes into a bowl, cover with hot water, and let soak for about 20 seconds, or until they become flexible. Remove them from the water and spread them out on the dish towel.

4 Take about 2 tablespoons of the bean sprout mixture and place on one of the pancakes toward the edge nearest you. Fold in the 2 sides, then the bottom edge so that it covers the filling. Roll it over again, holding in the filling firmly, and keep rolling until you have a firmly packed spring roll. Put it onto a plate, seam side down. Continue in this way until all the pancakes have been used. Cover the finished rolls with the clean, damp dish towel until required.

5 To make the dip, mix together the peanut butter, sugar, ginger, garlic, and red pepper flakes, then gradually mix in the soy sauce. Put into 4 small bowls and serve with the spring rolls.

Polenta fries with dipping sauces

You can make these fries quickly by using polenta tubes from larger supermarkets, Italian specialty stores, or online sources, or you can make the baked polenta—an Italian cornmeal dish—yourself.

SERVES 4

PREPARATION 15 MINUTES–1 HOUR, DEPENDING ON THE TYPE OF POLENTA OR CORNMEAL

COOKING 30 MINUTES–1¼ HOURS, DEPENDING ON THE POLENTA OR CORNMEAL

1 (18 oz) tube prepared polenta or 1 cup instant polenta or regular cornmeal
4 cups water
1 teaspoon salt
canola oil or peanut oil, for frying

FOR THE DIPPING SAUCES

¼ cup mayonnaise
1 tablespoon tomato paste
1 cup prepared chunky salsa
1 large ripe avocado
3 tablespoons chopped cilantro
juice of 1 lime
pinch of chili powder
salt and black pepper

1 If using the polenta tube, blot with paper towels, then cut into chunky fries—a tube will be enough to make about 24, then go to step 4.

2 Or, if using instant polenta, make as directed on the package. For traditional cornmeal, heat the water and salt in a large saucepan. When the water comes to a boil, sprinkle the cornmeal over the surface, stirring all the time to prevent lumps. If you do get some lumps, blend it with an immersion blender or wire whisk until smooth. Let the mixture simmer according to the package directions, until thick, stirring occasionally.

3 Line a 7 x 11 inch jellyroll pan with nonstick parchment paper. Pour the polenta or cornmeal into the pan, spreading it to the edges and into the corners. Let cool and become firm.

4 Meanwhile, make the dipping sauces. Mix the mayonnaise with the tomato paste and put into a small bowl. Put the salsa into another bowl. Remove the pit and skin from the avocado and mash the flesh with the cilantro, lime juice, chili powder, and some salt and black pepper to make a creamy, slightly chunky consistency. Put into a bowl.

5 Cut the firm polenta or cornmeal into fries about 6 inches long and ½ inch wide. Pour enough oil into a skillet to cover the fries and heat to 350–375°F, or until a cube of bread browns in 30 seconds, then pan-fry or deep-fry them. It's easy to keep them separate if you pan-fry them, but make sure they're submerged in oil and cook them until they are really crisp and golden on one side, then turn them over and cook the other side thoroughly. Drain on paper towels. If you get them crisp, the first batch will stay crisp while you fry the rest—keep them warm on paper towels in a cool oven.

6 Pile the fries into a stack on a serving dish—or on individual plates—and serve with the 3 dipping sauces.

Adzuki, rice & ginger balls with teriyaki dip ⓥ

MAKES 18
PREPARATION 20 MINUTES
COOKING 1 HOUR 5 MINUTES

¼ cup adzuki beans
⅔ cup brown rice
2 teaspoons grated fresh ginger root
1¼ cups water
2 teaspoons lemon juice
flesh from 2–3 umeboshi plums or
   1–2 teaspoons umeboshi paste
   (see page 296)
2–3 tablespoons sesame seeds
salt and black pepper

FOR THE DIP

3 tablespoons shoyu or tamari
3 tablespoons mirin

1　Put the beans into a saucepan, cover with water, and bring to a boil, then reduce the heat, cover the pan halfway, and simmer for 45 minutes, or until tender. Drain.

2　Meanwhile, put the rice and ginger into a saucepan with the measured water. Bring to a boil, then reduce the heat, cover, and let cook over gentle heat for 30–40 minutes, or until the rice is tender and all the water has been absorbed.

3　Put the rice into a food processor with the adzuki beans, lemon juice, umeboshi, and some salt and black pepper and process to a thick mixture that holds together.

4　Put the sesame seeds onto a large plate, then break off large marble-size pieces of the rice mixture and roll them in the seeds to form 18 balls. Place the rice balls on a baking sheet and bake in a preheated oven, at 350°F, for 20 minutes, or until crisp on the outside.

5　To make the dip, mix the shoyu or tamari with the mirin in a small bowl and serve with the rice balls.

Wild mushroom tempura with garlic mayonnaise ⓥ

Provided you buy a vegan mayonnaise, this makes a luxurious vegan main course—the unusual tempura batter is light and crisp. A package of mixed wild mushrooms from a supermarket is perfect for this recipe.

SERVES 4
PREPARATION 15 MINUTES
COOKING 30 MINUTES

1 lb mixed wild mushrooms,
   torn into bite-size pieces
canola oil or peanut oil, for
   deep-frying
garlic mayonnaise or aioli, to serve

FOR THE TEMPURA BATTER

¾ cup all-purpose white flour
1⅔ cups cornstarch
1 tablespoon baking powder
1 cup sparkling water
salt

1 Just before you want to serve the mushrooms, heat enough canola oil or peanut oil in a deep-fat fryer to 350–375°F, or until a cube of bread browns in 30 seconds.

2 While the oil is heating, make the batter. Put the flour, cornstarch, and baking powder into a bowl with some salt. Pour in the water and stir the mixture quickly with a fork or chopstick to make a batter.

3 Dip pieces of mushroom into the batter, then put them into the hot oil and deep-fry for 1–2 minutes, until they are golden brown and crisp. Drain on paper towels. You will need to cook in batches, but the first ones will stay crisp while you fry the rest.

4 Pile the tempura on a plate and serve immediately with the garlic mayonnaise or aioli.

Red pepper hummus with smoked paprika

Using sweet peppers from a jar makes this recipe quick and easy. Smoked paprika gives an intriguing, unusual flavor, but if you can't find it, use mild paprika instead.

SERVES 4

PREPARATION 15 MINUTES

2 garlic cloves

1 (15 oz) can chickpeas, drained

½ (12 oz) jar whole sweet red peppers, drained

1 teaspoon honey

Tabasco, to taste

¼–½ teaspoon smoked paprika

coarsely ground black pepper and warm grilled or toasted pita bread, to serve

1 Put the garlic cloves into a food processor and process until chopped, then add the chickpeas, red peppers, and honey and process again. Stir in the Tabasco and smoked paprika to taste.

2 Turn the mixture onto a flat plate and smooth the surface. Grind some black pepper coarsely over the top and serve with strips of warm grilled or toasted pita bread.

Fruity guacamole ⓥ

An authentic Mexican twist on an old favorite—a wonderful taste explosion of hot and salty, sweet and sour. This guacamole makes a wonderful appetizer, but you must prepare it just before serving for the best color.

SERVES 4
PREPARATION 25 MINUTES

1 large garlic clove
1 green chile, seeded
bunch of cilantro, stems removed
juice and pared or grated zest
    of 1 lime
2 ripe avocados, peeled, pitted,
    and coarsely chopped
1 pomegranate
1 ripe peach, peeled, pitted,
    and chopped
salt
2 small butterhead lettuce, leaves
    separated and hearts quartered,
    to serve

1 Put the garlic and chile into a food processor with most of the cilantro, saving a few cilantro leaves for garnishing. Process until finely chopped. Add the lime zest and juice (perhaps holding back a few strands of zest to garnish), the avocados, and a little salt and process to a green cream. Transfer to a mixing bowl.

2 Cut the pomegranate in half and bend back the skin—as if you were turning it inside out—to make the seeds pop out. Gently fold most of the seeds and the chopped peach into the avocado mixture.

3 Arrange the lettuce leaves and hearts around the edge of a serving dish. Pile the guacamole on top, then lightly stud it with the remaining peach and pomegranate and sprinkle with the reserved cilantro leaves and lime zest. Serve as soon as possible.

Refried beans

It's all the extras that make this simple dish special. I like to serve them in little bowls so everyone can help themselves to what they want.

SERVES 4
PREPARATION 15 MINUTES
COOKING 15 MINUTES

2 tablespoons olive oil
1 large onion, finely chopped
2 garlic cloves, chopped
2 (15 oz) cans pinto beans, drained
½–1 teaspoon chili powder
salt and black pepper

TO SERVE

lettuce leaves
sliced tomatoes
1 large avocado, peeled, pitted,
  and sliced
sour cream
paprika
chopped cilantro
tortilla chips
shredded cheddar cheese (optional)

1 Heat the olive oil in a large, heavy saucepan, add the onion, cover, and cook gently for 10 minutes, stirring from time to time. Stir in the garlic and cook for a minute or two longer.

2 Add the pinto beans to the pan, along with the chili powder, salt, and black pepper to taste. Mash the beans coarsely with a potato masher or wooden spoon so that they cling together but keep plenty of texture. Stir well so that they don't stick to the pan. The beans are ready when they're piping hot.

3 Arrange some lettuce leaves on a large serving plate and spoon the beans into the center. Arrange tomato and avocado slices around the edge, swirl sour cream, paprika, and cilantro on top, and serve with tortilla chips and shredded cheddar, if desired.

Stilton pâté with roasted baby beets, dill & endive salad

SERVES 4
PREPARATION 15 MINUTES
COOKING 1–1½ HOURS

1 lb baby beets, preferably no bigger
   than plums
olive oil, for rubbing
dill sprigs, to garnish
coarsely ground black pepper and
   rustic bread, to serve

FOR THE STILTON PÂTÉ

1 cup low-fat cream cheese
1 teaspoon Dijon mustard
8 oz Stilton cheese, coarsely crumbled
1 tablespoon vegetarian port
   or sweet sherry
black pepper

FOR THE SALAD

2–3 heads of endive
bunch of watercress
½ cup walnuts

1 If the beets still have leaves attached, cut them off about 2 inches from the beet. Scrub the beets gently, being careful not to pierce the skin, and leave the long "tail" on, if still attached. Rub the beets with a little olive oil, wrap them lightly in a piece of aluminum foil and bake in a preheated oven, at 400°F, for 1–1½ hours, or until tender right through when pierced with a knife. You could uncover them for the last 30 minutes or so, but you don't want them to get too crisp. I like to eat them skins and all, but most people rub off the skins before eating.

2 While the beets are cooking, make the pâté. Put the cream cheese, mustard, Stilton, and port or sherry into a food processor and process to a cream. Season with a little black pepper.

3 Mix together the ingredients for the salad.

4 To serve, put a spoonful of the Stilton pâté on each plate with some of the beets—baby ones can be left whole, larger ones cut as necessary—and one or two feathery leaves of dill. Grind some black pepper coarsely over the top and serve with the salad and rustic bread.

Nut & miso pâté with cranberry relish & dill ⓥ

This wonderful and unusual pâté was inspired by a recipe that appeared in the *Vegetarian Times*. Serve with strips of warm pita bread.

SERVES 4
PREPARATION 20 MINUTES,
   PLUS SOAKING
COOKING 15 MINUTES

½ cup cashew nuts
4 oz firm tofu, drained
1 garlic clove, crushed
4 teaspoons red miso
1 tablespoon nutritional yeast
   (see page 295) **or a little yeast**
   extract, to taste
1 teaspoon shoyu or tamari
4 teaspoons lemon juice
white pepper
3 tablespoons chopped dill
4 dill sprigs, to garnish

FOR THE CRANBERRY RELISH

⅓ cup dried cranberries
⅔ cup full-bodied red wine
1 teaspoon olive oil
¼ teaspoon white mustard seeds
1 tablespoon finely chopped onion
1 garlic clove, finely chopped
1 teaspoon grated fresh ginger root
pinch of chili powder
1 tablespoon granulated sugar
1 tablespoon red wine vinegar
salt

1 First make the cranberry relish. Put the cranberries into a bowl, cover with the wine, and set aside. Heat the olive oil in a small saucepan, add the mustard seeds, stir for a few seconds until they start to "pop," then add the onion, garlic, ginger, and chili powder. Cook over gentle heat for about 5 minutes, or until the onion is tender.

2 Add the cranberries and their liquid to the pan, along with the sugar, red wine vinegar, and some salt. Bring to a boil, then reduce the heat and simmer, uncovered, for a few minutes, until the liquid has reduced and is syrupy and the cranberries are tender. Cool. (This will keep, covered, in the refrigerator for up to 2 weeks.)

3 For the pâté, put the cashews into a bowl, cover with cold water, and let soak for 4–8 hours. Drain. Put into a food processor with the tofu, garlic, miso, yeast, shoyu or tamari, lemon juice, and a good pinch of white pepper and process to a creamy pâté. Scrape into a bowl, cover, and set aside until required.

4 To serve, stir the chopped dill and ¼ cup of the cranberry relish into the pâté. Arrange a spoonful in the center of each of 4 plates and garnish each with a dill sprig. Serve at once—the pâté loses its bright, fresh color if left to stand.

Lentil & olive pâté with broiled fennel ⓥ

SERVES 4
PREPARATION 10 MINUTES
COOKING 10 MINUTES

4 fennel bulbs
2 tablespoons olive oil
lemon wedges, to serve

FOR THE PÂTÉ

2 garlic cloves
1 (15 oz) can green lentils, drained,
  or 2 cups cooked green lentils
1½ cups pitted, ripe black olives,
  such as Kalamata

1 Trim the tops off the fennel, then, using a sharp knife or a potato peeler, shave off a thin layer of the outer bracts to remove any tough threads. Cut the bulbs in half, then into quarters or sixths, depending on the size of the fennel. Brush the pieces on both sides with olive oil, place on a broiler pan, and cook under a preheated hot broiler for about 10 minutes, or until tender and browned, turning them as necessary.

2 Meanwhile, make the pâté. Put the garlic cloves into a food processor and process to chop, then add the lentils and black olives and process again to a thick, fairly chunky consistency.

3 Heap the pâté up on a plate, arrange the broiled fennel and lemon wedges around the edge, and serve.

Soups & salads

Red lentil & roasted red pepper soup

SERVES 6
PREPARATION 20 MINUTES
COOKING 40 MINUTES

2 red onions, cut into 1 inch pieces
2 teaspoons olive oil
2 red bell peppers, halved, cored,
   and seeded
4 garlic cloves, unpeeled
small handful of thyme
⅔ cup split red lentils
2½ cups water
2 bay leaves
salt and black pepper
chopped basil, to garnish
a few shavings of Parmesan-style
   cheese, to serve

1 Toss the onions in the olive oil and put them on a baking sheet, along with the red bell peppers, which don't need oiling. Roast in a preheated oven, at 350°F, for 30 minutes, or until the vegetables are nearly tender, then add the garlic and thyme to the baking sheet and cook for another 10 minutes, until all the vegetables are tender. Let cool.

2 Meanwhile, put the red lentils into a saucepan with the water and bay leaves. Bring to a boil, then reduce the heat and simmer for 15 minutes, or until the lentils are soft and pale. Remove and discard the bay leaves.

3 Rub off as much of the skin from the red peppers as you can—get rid of any dark sections, but don't worry about being too particular. Pop the garlic out of its skin with your fingers. Put the red peppers and garlic into a food processor with the onion (discard the thyme). Add the lentils together with their cooking liquid and process to a smooth, creamy consistency, thinning it with a little water, if necessary.

4 Return the mixture to the pan and reheat gently. Season to taste with salt and black pepper, then ladle into warmed bowls and top each with basil and thin shavings of Parmesan.

Hot & sour mushroom soup ⓥ

This glamorous soup has a long list of ingredients, but is incredibly quick to make. Use a medium, long chile for this soup—not the tiny, very hot type of chile. Make sure the curry paste is vegetarian—read the label.

SERVES 4
PREPARATION 10 MINUTES,
   PLUS STANDING
COOKING 15–20 MINUTES

1 teaspoon vegetarian Thai red
   curry paste
4 oz shiitake mushrooms, thinly sliced
1 small cluster of enoki mushrooms,
   bottom trimmed off
1 red chile, seeded and cut into rings
½ cup chopped cilantro
juice of 1 lime
2–3 tablespoons shoyu or tamari
salt

FOR THE THAI-FLAVORED STOCK

2–3 lemon grass stalks, crushed
   with a rolling pin
6 kaffir lime leaves, plus 6 more to
   garnish (optional)
stems from a small bunch of cilantro
2 thumb-size pieces of fresh
   ginger root, peeled and sliced
4 cups water

1 To make the stock, put the lemon grass, lime leaves, cilantro stems, and ginger into a saucepan with the water. Bring to a boil, then reduce the heat and simmer for 10 minutes. Remove from the heat, cover the pan, and let stand for 30 minutes or longer for the flavors to steep, then drain the liquid into another pan and discard the flavorings.

2 Add the curry paste, mushrooms, and red chile to the stock, then reheat and simmer for 3–4 minutes, to cook the mushrooms and chile.

3 Stir in the chopped cilantro, lime juice, shoyu or tamari, and some salt, then heat gently. Ladle into warmed bowls and garnish with a lime leaf, if desired.

Carrot & caraway soup ⓥ

Caraway, from the same plant family as carrots, gives this soup its subtle, unusual flavor and deserves to be more widely used. It also adds a wonderful flavor to cooked, buttered carrots or beets.

SERVES 4
PREPARATION 15 MINUTES
COOKING 40 MINUTES

1 tablespoon olive oil
1 onion, chopped
1 baking potato, peeled and cut into
    ½ inch cubes
1 lb carrots, cleaned and sliced
    (about 4 cups)
2–3 strips of lemon zest
1 teaspoon caraway seeds
5 cups water or light vegetable stock
salt and black pepper
fromage blanc, plain Greek yogurt, or
    reduced-fat crème fraîche
    (optional) and coarsely ground black
    pepper, to serve
chopped flat leaf parsley, to garnish

1 Heat the olive oil in a large saucepan, add the onion, cover, and cook gently for 5 minutes, stirring from time to time; don't let it brown.

2 Add the potato, cover, and cook for another 5 minutes, then add the carrots, lemon zest, and caraway seeds. Stir well, then add the water or stock. Bring to a boil, then reduce the heat, cover, and let cook gently for about 30 minutes, or until the carrots are tender.

3 Puree the soup in a food processor or blender, then return the mixture to the pan. Season with plenty of salt and a little black pepper and reheat gently.

4 Ladle the soup into warmed bowls and swirl a teaspoon of fromage blanc, yogurt, or crème fraîche on top of each, if desired. Grind some black pepper coarsely over the top, sprinkle with a little flat leaf parsley, and serve.

Chunky bean & vegetable soup ⓥ

There are numerous versions of this Mediterranean soup, which is easy to make and deliciously wholesome. Feel free to try using different vegetables or perhaps adding some small pasta shapes.

SERVES 4
PREPARATION 15 MINUTES
COOKING 45 MINUTES

1 tablespoon olive oil
2 onions, chopped
4 carrots, cut into ½ inch chunks
2 parsnips, cut into ½ inch chunks
3 leeks, sliced
3 cups sliced cabbage
a few thyme sprigs
2 bay leaves
1 (15 oz) can cannellini beans, drained
5 cups vegetable stock
salt and black pepper
chopped parsley, to garnish
whole-wheat bread and grated cheese,
    to serve (optional)

1 Heat the olive oil in a large saucepan, add the onions, cover, and cook for 5 minutes. Add the carrots, parsnips, leeks, cabbage, thyme, and bay leaves and stir to lightly coat them all with the oil. Cover and cook gently for another 10 minutes.

2 Add the beans and stock, bring to a boil, then reduce the heat, cover, and let simmer over gentle heat for 30 minutes. Season with salt and black pepper, then ladle into warmed bowls and top each with a sprinkling of chopped parsley. Serve with whole-wheat bread and grated cheese, if desired.

Creamy fennel soup with gremolata

SERVES 4
PREPARATION 15 MINUTES
COOKING 20 MINUTES

2 large fennel bulbs, trimmed
   and sliced
1 onion, coarsely chopped
4 cups vegetable stock
⅓ cup heavy cream
salt and black pepper

FOR THE GREMOLATA

2 tablespoons chopped parsley
thinly pared or finely grated zest
   of ½ lemon
1 garlic clove, finely chopped

1 Put the fennel and onion into a saucepan with the stock. Bring to a boil, then reduce the heat and gently simmer for 15–20 minutes, until tender.

2 To make the gremolata, mix all the ingredients in a bowl and set aside.

3 Puree the fennel mixture in a food processor or using an immersion blender until smooth. If you prefer an even smoother texture, pass the soup through a strainer into a clean pan.

4 Add the cream to the soup and season with salt and black pepper, then ladle into warmed bowls and top each with a spoonful of gremolata.

Butternut squash & orange soup with nutmeg •ⱽ

SERVES 4
PREPARATION 15 MINUTES
COOKING 35 MINUTES

1 butternut squash, halved
   and seeded
2 tablespoons olive oil, plus extra
   for greasing
2 onions, chopped
2 garlic cloves, chopped
juice and grated zest of 1 orange
¼ teaspoon ground nutmeg
4 cups water
salt and black pepper
chopped parsley, to garnish

1 Put the squash, cut side down, on a lightly oiled baking sheet and bake in a preheated oven, at 400°F, for 30 minutes, or until tender.

2 Meanwhile, heat the olive oil in a large, heavy saucepan, add the onions, cover, and cook over gentle heat for about 10 minutes, until tender. Stir in the garlic and cook for a minute or two longer.

3 Scoop out the flesh from the butternut squash halves and mix with the onions and garlic, orange juice and zest, nutmeg, and some salt and black pepper. Puree using an immersion blender or food processor, adding a little of the water, if necessary.

4 Transfer the mixture to a saucepan with enough of the water to make a creamy consistency and heat gently.

5 Ladle the soup into warmed bowls and serve garnished with chopped parsley.

Iced beet soup

This soup, which you can also serve hot if you prefer, brought me a marriage proposal. It's particularly effective served in bowls sitting in outer bowls of crushed ice.

SERVES 6
PREPARATION 25 MINUTES,
   PLUS CHILLING
COOKING 30–40 MINUTES

1 tablespoon olive oil
1 large onion, chopped
1 large potato, peeled and cut into
   small cubes
5 cups coarsely diced cooked beets
   (not in vinegar)
pared zest of ½ lemon
6 cups water or light vegetable stock
2 tablespoons lemon juice
salt and black pepper
chives, dill, or mint, to garnish
sour cream and coarsely ground
   black pepper, to serve

1 Heat the olive oil in a large saucepan, add the onion, and sauté for 10 minutes, until soft but not brown, then add the potato, cover, and cook gently for another 5 minutes.

2 Add the beets, lemon zest, and water or stock. Bring to a boil, then reduce the heat, cover, and simmer for 15–20 minutes, or until the potato is soft.

3 Puree the mixture in a food processor or blender until perfectly smooth. If you prefer an even smoother texture, pass the mixture through a strainer into a large bowl.

4 Add the lemon juice and season with salt and black pepper to taste. Chill until required, then taste and adjust the seasoning, if necessary.

5 To serve, ladle the soup into chilled bowls and top with a spoonful of sour cream, some coarsely ground black pepper, and herbs of your choice.

Chilled melon soup with mint granita ⓥ

SERVES 4
PREPARATION 20 MINUTES,
  PLUS CHILLING AND FREEZING
COOKING 5 MINUTES

1 ripe honeydew melon
granulated sugar, to taste

FOR THE MINT GRANITA

⅔ cup granulated sugar
large bunch of mint
1¼ cups water
1 tablespoon lemon juice

1   Remove the skin and seeds from the melon and cut the flesh into chunks. Puree in a food processor until smooth. Taste and add a little sugar, if necessary, then chill.

2   To make the granita, put the sugar, mint, and water into a saucepan and heat gently until the sugar has dissolved, then bring to a boil. Remove from the heat, cover, and let stand until cold.

3   Once cold, remove the mint and squeeze it to extract all the liquid. Save about a dozen leaves and discard the rest. Puree the liquid with the reserved leaves and add the lemon juice. Pour into a freezer-proof container and freeze until firm. Remove from the freezer 20–30 minutes before you want to serve it to let the granita soften a little.

4   To serve, ladle the melon soup into chilled bowls. Beat the frozen mint mixture with a fork (or process chunks briefly in a food processor) and add a scoop to each bowl. Serve at once.

Hot pomegranate & pecan leafy salad ⓥ

SERVES 4
PREPARATION 10 MINUTES
COOKING 12 MINUTES

1 cup coarsely broken pecans
1 tablespoon balsamic vinegar
2 tablespoons olive oil
1 (8 oz) package peppery greens, such
    as arugula or watercress
1 pomegranate
salt and black pepper

1 Spread out the pecans on a baking sheet and place in a preheated oven, at 350°F, for about 12 minutes, or until lightly browned and aromatic. Remove from the oven and transfer to a plate to prevent them from burning.

2 Mix the balsamic vinegar, olive oil, and some salt and black pepper in a large salad bowl to make a dressing.

3 Put the salad greens on top of the dressing, but don't toss them. Cut the pomegranate in half and bend back the skin—as if you were turning it inside out—to make the seeds pop out. Add the seeds to the leaves, along with the pecans.

4 Toss the salad and serve immediately.

Wakame, cucumber & scallion salad with rice vinegar ⓥ

SERVES 4
PREPARATION 10 MINUTES, PLUS
   SOAKING

¼ oz wakame seaweed
½ cucumber, peeled and shredded
6 scallions, chopped
1 tablespoon rice vinegar
1 tablespoon mirin (or a dash of honey
   for nonvegans)
1 tablespoon shoyu or tamari
sugar, to taste
a few toasted sesame seeds
salt and black pepper

1   Put the wakame into a bowl, cover with boiling water, and let soak for 10 minutes, then drain and chop or snip.

2   Put the cucumber and scallions into a bowl. Add the wakame, rice vinegar, mirin or honey, and the shoyu or tamari, mix gently, and season with salt, black pepper, and sugar to taste.

3   Put the salad into a shallow dish or onto individual plates and sprinkle with a few toasted sesame seeds. Serve at once.

Arugula, avocado & pine nut salad

Some fresh, warm walnut or rye bread will make the perfect accompaniment for this summer salad.

SERVES 4
PREPARATION 10 MINUTES

1 tablespoon balsamic vinegar
2 tablespoons olive oil
8 sun-dried tomatoes, chopped
⅓ cup raisins
2 (5 oz) packages arugula
8 oz vegetarian Pecorino
  cheese or Parmesan-style cheese,
  shaved or thinly sliced
¼ cup pine nuts, lightly toasted
1 large avocado, peeled, pitted, and cut
  into chunks
black pepper
warm crusty bread, to serve

1 Put the balsamic vinegar, olive oil and pepper to taste into a large serving bowl and beat together with a spoon until combined.

2 Add the tomatoes, raisins, arugula, Pecorino, pine nuts, and avocado and toss everything together. Serve with warmed bread.

Quinoa & red grape salad with honey dressing & toasted almonds

SERVES 4
PREPARATION 15 MINUTES
COOKING 20 MINUTES

1 cup quinoa
2 cups water
2 tablespoons slivered almonds
2 cups halved seedless red grapes
3–4 scallions, chopped
4 teaspoons honey
4 teaspoons cider vinegar
salt and black pepper
butterhead lettuce leaves, to serve

1 Put the quinoa into a saucepan with the water. Bring to a boil, then reduce the heat, cover, and cook gently for 15 minutes, until the quinoa is tender. Remove from the heat and let stand, covered, for a few more minutes, or until cold.

2 Spread out the slivered almonds on a broiler pan or shallow roasting pan that will fit under the broiler. Cook under a preheated hot broiler for a minute or so until they turn golden. Give them a stir, if necessary, so they cook evenly, but watch them like a hawk because they burn easily. As soon as they're done, remove them from the broiler and transfer to a plate to make sure they don't continue cooking in the residual heat.

3 Put the quinoa into a bowl with the grapes, scallions, honey, cider vinegar, and some salt and black pepper and mix gently. This can be done in advance, if you desire.

4 Just before serving, stir in the slivered almonds. It's especially nice if they're still slightly warm from the broiler. Serve with some crunchy butterhead lettuce leaves.

Lemon-glazed & seared haloumi with herb salad

The haloumi, available in health-food stores or online, can be marinated well in advance, but cook it quickly at the last minute so that it is light and delicious.

SERVES 4
PREPARATION 10 MINUTES, PLUS
   MARINATING
COOKING 5–10 MINUTES

2 (8 oz) packages haloumi cheese,
   drained, or Muenster cheese
¼ cup lemon juice
2 tablespoons honey

FOR THE HERB SALAD

1 (8 oz) package mixed baby greens
   and herb salad
2 tablespoons olive oil
salt and black pepper

1 Cut the cheese into slices about ¼ inch thick. Put them on a plate in a single layer.

2 Mix the lemon juice with the honey and pour it over the haloumi, turning to coat the slices all over. Let marinate for at least 1 hour.

3 When you are ready to serve, toss the greens with the olive oil and some salt and black pepper and divide among 4 plates.

4 Put the slices of cheese into a dry skillet over moderate heat, reserving any liquid. Cook until golden brown, then flip them over and cook the other side. This is a quick process because they cook fast. When cooked, pour in any liquid that was left from the marinade and let simmer until it has mostly evaporated and becomes a sweet glaze.

5 Arrange the slices of cheese on top of the salad and serve at once.

Lima bean salad with sweet chili dressing ⓥ

SERVES 4

PREPARATION 5 MINUTES

2 (15 oz) cans lima beans,
   drained and rinsed
1 teaspoon dried crushed red peppers
2 teaspoons maple syrup
2 tablespoons rice vinegar
2 teaspoons toasted sesame oil
2 teaspoons shoyu or tamari
2 scallions, thinly sliced
3–4 tablespoons coarsely chopped
   celery leaves
⅓ cup salted peanuts, crushed
black pepper

1 Put the lima beans into a bowl, add the crushed red peppers, maple syrup, rice vinegar, sesame oil, shoyu or tamari, and a grinding of pepper and stir gently to mix.

2 Add the scallions and celery leaves, then stir again. Add the crushed peanuts just before serving, so that they remain crisp.

Warm baby broccoli Caesar with toasted almonds

Use a homemade lemon mayonnaise (see page 160) or a good-quality store-bought one as the basis of the dressing. I pep up the flavor with Tabasco instead of Worcestershire sauce, which contains anchovy essence.

SERVES 4
PREPARATION 15 MINUTES
COOKING 4–5 MINUTES

1 (8 oz) package baby broccoli
   (broccolini), trimmed
1 romaine lettuce, outer leaves
   removed, or 2 lettuce hearts

FOR THE DRESSING

¼ cup mayonnaise
1 tablespoon lemon juice
Tabasco, to taste
⅓ cup Parmesan-style cheese shavings
2 tablespoons toasted slivered almonds
salt and black pepper

1 Cook the broccoli in a saucepan of boiling water for 4–5 minutes, or until just tender—the time will depend on the thickness of the stems. Drain.

2 Meanwhile, make the dressing. Mix together the mayonnaise, lemon juice, and enough Tabasco to give it a good zing. Season with salt and black pepper and stir in half the Parmesan.

3 Tear the lettuce into pieces and put into a bowl with the broccoli. Pour the dressing over and toss lightly. Top with the remaining Parmesan and the almonds and serve immediately.

Stilton & cherry salad
with cinnamon dressing

I adapted this salad from one served by Chef Robert Bruce in New Orleans. It has a particularly warming, festive feel.

SERVES 4

PREPARATION 10 MINUTES,
   PLUS MARINATING

⅓ cup dried cherries

2 tablespoons sherry, port, or other
   fortified wine

1 large lettuce, torn, or about 1 lb
   mixed salad greens

2 oz Stilton or other blue cheese,
   crumbled

½ cup toasted slivered almonds

FOR THE CINNAMON DRESSING

¼ cup olive oil

2 tablespoons raspberry vinegar

2 teaspoons granulated sugar

1 teaspoon ground cinnamon

Tabasco, to taste

salt and black pepper

1 Put the dried cherries into a small bowl, cover with the sherry or port, and set aside until plump—if you can let them stand for a few hours, so much the better.

2 To make the dressing, whisk together the olive oil, raspberry vinegar, sugar, cinnamon, and several drops of Tabasco—enough to give it a good kick—and some salt and black pepper.

3 Put the lettuce or salad greens into a bowl with the Stilton, almonds, and cherries, together with any of their remaining liquid. Drizzle with the cinnamon dressing and toss gently. Serve at once.

Salad of warm artichokes & chanterelles

Provided you have a couple of large saucepans, I think it's easier to cook the artichokes whole and then remove the leaves and choke instead of first trimming them.

SERVES 4
PREPARATION 30 MINUTES
COOKING 50 MINUTES

4 globe artichokes, stems removed
2 tablespoons olive oil
2 tablespoons butter
8 oz chanterelle mushrooms
4 garlic cloves, finely chopped
squeeze of lemon juice
1 head of frilly red-leafed lettuce
salt and black pepper
chopped chives, to garnish

FOR THE VINAIGRETTE DRESSING

2 tablespoons balsamic vinegar
⅓ cup extra virgin olive oil

1 Cook the artichokes in a saucepan of boiling water for about 45 minutes, or until a leaf will pull off easily. Drain and rinse under cold water to cool quickly. Pull off the leaves until you get to the central fluffy "choke," then pull this off gently with your fingers under cold running water and discard. Slice the bottoms thickly and set aside.

2 To make the dressing, put the balsamic vinegar, olive oil, and a generous seasoning of salt into a lidded jar and shake until combined.

3 Just before you want to serve the salad, heat the olive oil and butter in a skillet, add the chanterelles and garlic, and cook for a few minutes, until they are tender and any liquid has been reabsorbed. Add the sliced artichoke bases and cook for 1–2 minutes to heat them through, stirring often. Season well with a squeeze of lemon juice and some salt and black pepper.

4 While the mushrooms are cooking, arrange some lettuce leaves on 4 plates and drizzle with the dressing. Spoon the chanterelle and artichoke mixture on top and sprinkle with chopped chives. Serve immediately.

Thai-flavored slaw ◉

This salad can be made in advance, if you prefer; the cabbage will soften in the tasty, oil-free dressing.

SERVES 4
PREPARATION 10 MINUTES
COOKING 2–3 MINUTES

½ small head of cabbage, about 9 oz
small bunch of cilantro,
    coarsely chopped
4 scallions, chopped
1 mild red chile, seeded and chopped
2 tablespoons rice vinegar
1 tablespoon mirin or 1 teaspoon
    honey
1 tablespoon sesame seeds
salt

1 Cut the cabbage in half, cut away and discard the hard inner core, then shred the cabbage finely with a sharp knife and put into a bowl.

2 To make the light dressing, add the cilantro, scallions, and chile to the bowl, stir in the rice vinegar and mirin or honey, and season with salt.

3 Toast the sesame seeds by putting them into a small, dry saucepan and stirring over moderate heat for a minute or two until they begin to turn golden brown and smell delicious, then sprinkle them over the salad.

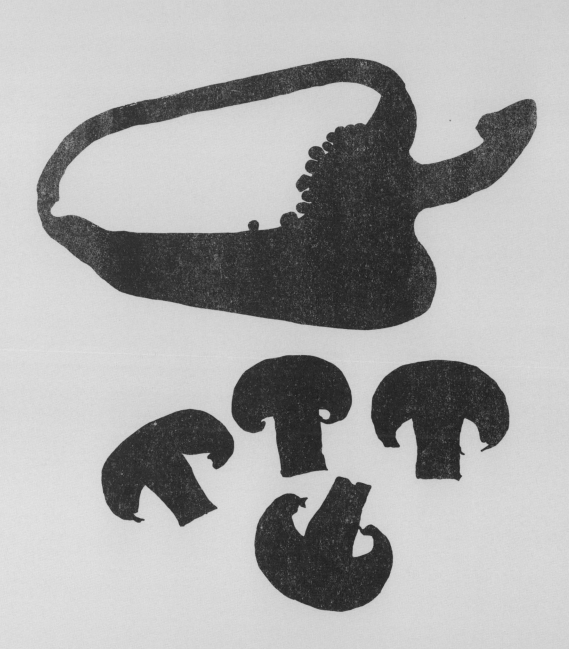

Classics with a twist

Thai-flavored mushroom stroganoff with golden rice ⓥ

For a lighter version, use half coconut milk and half water, which is better value than buying "light" coconut milk where you're simply paying for the water—read the ingredients on the label.

SERVES 4
PREPARATION 15 MINUTES
COOKING 20 MINUTES

1 tablespoon canola oil
1 lb baby mushrooms, halved
   or quartered, depending on size
2 lemon grass stalks, crushed
4–6 lime leaves or the grated zest
   of 1 lime
1 tablespoon grated fresh ginger root
4 teaspoons cornstarch
3⅓ cups coconut milk
salt and black pepper
¼ cup coarsely chopped
   cilantro leaves, to garnish

FOR THE RICE

1½ cups white basmati rice or
   other long-grain rice
pinch of turmeric
2½ cups water

1 Start with the rice. Put it into a heavy saucepan with the turmeric, a little salt, if you desire, and the water. Bring to a boil, then cover, reduce the heat, and let cook gently for 15 minutes, or until the rice is tender and the water has been absorbed. Fluff with a fork and keep warm, covered, until required.

2 Meanwhile, heat the canola oil in a large saucepan, add the mushrooms, stir, cover, and cook for about 5 minutes, or until tender.

3 Add the lemon grass, lime leaves or zest, and ginger and stir over the heat for a few seconds to release the flavors.

4 Blend the cornstarch to a thin paste with a little of the coconut milk and set aside. Add the remaining coconut milk to the mushrooms, bring to a boil, then reduce the heat and simmer for 5 minutes. Pour in the cornstarch paste, bring to a boil, and stir for a minute or so as it thickens. Season with salt and black pepper, then remove the lemon grass (and, if you desire, the lime leaves, if using).

5 Serve the stroganoff with the hot cooked rice topped with the cilantro.

Tamari-flavored nut roast with tomato sauce

Start this recipe by making the tomato sauce. Use some of it in the nut roast mixture and serve the rest of the sauce with the cooked nut roast.

SERVES 4
PREPARATION 40 MINUTES
COOKING 1½ HOURS

1 tablespoon olive oil
1 large onion, chopped
4 garlic cloves, finely chopped
2 (14½ oz) cans diced tomatoes
½ cup basil
2 cups chopped mushrooms
3 cups soft whole-wheat
   bread crumbs
1 cup chopped pecans
1¼ cups ground almonds
   (almond meal)
1 tablespoon tamari
½ teaspoon yeast extract
1 egg
salt and black pepper

1 Heat the olive oil in a large, heavy saucepan, add the onion, cover, and cook gently for 10 minutes, stirring from time to time. Stir in the garlic and cook for a minute or two longer, then add the tomatoes. Cook, uncovered, for about 20 minutes, or until the liquid has disappeared and the mixture is thick.

2 Meanwhile, remove one good sprig of basil for garnishing and set aside; coarsely chop the rest.

3 Put half the tomato mixture into a large bowl and add the chopped basil, mushrooms, bread crumbs, pecans, ground almonds, tamari, yeast extract, and egg. Mix well and season with salt and black pepper.

4 Line a 8½ x 4½ x 2½ inch loaf pan with a strip of nonstick parchment paper to cover the bottom and wide sides. Spoon the mixture into the pan, smooth the surface, and cover lightly with another piece of nonstick parchment paper. Bake in a preheated oven, at 350°F, for 1 hour.

5 Let the nut roast stand for 3–4 minutes to settle while you reheat the remaining tomato mixture and season it with salt and black pepper. You could thin it with a little water for a pouring consistency, if you desire, or leave it chunky.

6 Slip a knife around the edges of the nut roast, turn it out, and strip off the paper. Garnish with the reserved basil sprig and serve in thick slices, accompanied by the tomato sauce.

Falafel with lemon sauce ⓥ

I generally use canned beans for speed when cooking, but this is one recipe where you need to use dried ones for an authentic result.

SERVES 4
PREPARATION 15 MINUTES,
   PLUS SOAKING
COOKING 15 MINUTES

1½ cups dried chickpeas
1 small onion, coarsely chopped
⅓ cup coarsely chopped cilantro
2 garlic cloves, coarsely chopped
1 tablespoon ground cumin
½ teaspoon baking soda
1½ teaspoons salt
2 tablespoons chickpea (besan) flour
canola oil, for pan-frying

FOR THE LEMON SAUCE

¼ cup plain yogurt (dairy or vegan)
¼ cup good-quality mayonnaise
   (dairy or vegan)
grated zest of ½ lemon
1–2 tablespoons lemon juice

TO SERVE

warmed, halved pita bread
shredded lettuce
sliced tomato
sliced cucumber
sliced onion
mint leaves, chopped
shredded carrot (optional)

1 Put the chickpeas into a saucepan, cover with plenty of water, and bring to a boil. Boil for 2 minutes, then let soak for 1–2 hours. (Alternatively, just soak them overnight.) Drain.

2 Put the drained chickpeas into a food processor with the onion, cilantro, garlic, cumin, baking soda, and salt and process until the ingredients are finely ground and hold together.

3 Take a small handful of the mixture and squeeze it between your palms to extract any excess liquid. Repeat until you've used up all the mixture, then coat the falafels lightly in flour.

4 Heat a little canola oil in a skillet and cook the falafel on all sides until brown and crisp. Drain on paper towels.

5 To make the sauce, simply mix together all the ingredients. Serve the falafel with the warmed pita bread; let people fill the pita halves with a selection of hot falafels, salad ingredients, and lemon sauce.

No-rice nori sushi ⓥ

MAKES 16–20
PREPARATION 20 MINUTES

2 daikon (Asian radishes) or
    4–5 turnips (about 1½ lb),
    peeled and shredded
2 teaspoons rice vinegar or
    wine vinegar
2 teaspoons sugar
4–5 pieces of nori seaweed
1 red bell pepper, cored, seeded,
    and cut into long strips
½ cucumber, peeled and cut
    into long strips
1 avocado, peeled, pitted, and cut
    into long strips
salt and black pepper
toasted sesame seeds, to garnish
    (optional)
wasabi paste and pickled ginger,
    to serve

FOR THE SOY SAUCE DIP

2 tablespoons soy sauce
2 tablespoons mirin
2 tablespoons sake

1 To make the dip, mix together the soy sauce, mirin, and sake. Put into a small serving bowl and set aside.

2 Squeeze the daikon or turnips with your hands to extract as much moisture as possible (you need a fairly dry mixture). Mix in the vinegar and sugar and add salt and black pepper to taste.

3 Place a piece of nori, shiny side down, on a board and cover it lightly with the daikon or turnip mixture, leaving a ½ inch gap at the end farthest from you. Squeeze out any extra liquid, as necessary.

4 Put a row of red bell pepper strips on top, at the end closest to you, about 1 inch from the edge. Place a thin line of cucumber and one of avocado next to the red bell pepper. Fold over the end closest to you, quite firmly, then continue to roll the nori up, like a jellyroll. Continue in the same way until all the ingredients have been used. Chill until required.

5 To serve, trim the ends of each roll—these tend to be a little untidy— then cut the rolls into 4 pieces and put them, filling side up, on a serving plate. Sprinkle with a few sesame seeds, if desired. Serve with the soy sauce dip, a little bowl of wasabi paste, and some pickled ginger.

Omelet cannelloni with spinach filling

This is delicious—an excellent dish if you're trying to lose weight, whether you're counting calories or carbs.

SERVES 4
PREPARATION 20 MINUTES
COOKING 40 MINUTES

2 (10 oz) packages fresh spinach
½ cup low-fat soft cream cheese
½ cup grated Parmesan-style cheese
grated nutmeg
4 eggs
2 tablespoons water
1 tablespoon olive oil
salt and black pepper

1 Wash the spinach, then place in a large saucepan with just the water clinging to the leaves, cover, and cook for 6–7 minutes, or until tender. Drain well.

2 Add the cream cheese to the spinach along with ¼ cup of the Parmesan cheese. Mix well and season with salt, black pepper, and grated nutmeg. Set aside.

3 Whisk the eggs with the water and salt and black pepper to taste. Brush a skillet (preferably nonstick) with a little of the olive oil and heat, then pour in enough of the egg—about 2 tablespoons—to make a small omelet. Cook for a few seconds, until it is set, then lift out onto a plate. Continue in this way until you have made about 8 small omelets, piling them up on top of each other.

4 Spoon a little of the spinach mixture onto the edge of one of the omelets, roll it up, and place in a shallow gratin dish. Fill the remaining omelets in the same way, until all the spinach mixture is used, placing them snugly side by side in the dish. Sprinkle with the remaining Parmesan and bake in a preheated oven, at 375°F, for about 25 minutes, or until bubbling and golden brown on top.

Vegetarian pad thai

You can buy deep-fried tofu, or make your own by cutting the tofu into cubes and deep-frying in a little canola oil or peanut oil for about 5 minutes, until golden brown.

SERVES 4
PREPARATION 20 MINUTES
COOKING 20 MINUTES

8 oz rice noodles
canola oil, for deep-frying
1 lb firm tofu, drained and cut
    into ½ inch cubes
2 tablespoons toasted sesame oil
2 onions, chopped
4 garlic cloves, finely chopped
4 teaspoons tamarind puree
2 tablespoons soy sauce
2 teaspoons packed brown sugar
1¼ cups bean sprouts
2 eggs, beaten
¼–⅓ cup roasted peanuts,
    lightly crushed
salt and black pepper
coarsely chopped cilantro, to garnish
lime wedges, to serve

1 Put the noodles into a bowl, cover with boiling water, and let soak until tender, according to the package directions; the timing depends on the thickness of the noodles; fine ones take 5 minutes, thicker ones take longer. Drain.

2 Heat the canola oil in a wok to 350–375°F or until a cube of bread browns in 30 seconds. Add the tofu and deep-fry for about 5 minutes. Drain on paper towels.

3 Heat all but 1 teaspoon of the sesame oil in a large saucepan, add the onions, and sauté for 7–10 minutes, until tender, then stir in the garlic. Cook for a few seconds, then stir in the deep-fried tofu, tamarind puree, soy sauce, brown sugar, bean sprouts, and drained noodles. Cook over the heat for 2–3 minutes, until the bean sprouts are tender and everything is heated through.

4 Meanwhile, heat the remaining sesame oil in a skillet, pour in the eggs, and make an omelet, pulling back the edges of the omelet as it sets and tipping the pan so that uncooked egg runs to the edges. When the omelet is set, roll it up, put it on a plate, cut into shreds, and add to the noodles.

5 Season the noodle mixture to taste with salt and black pepper, then serve on warmed plates and top with the crushed peanuts and a generous amount of cilantro and serve with lime wedges.

Creamy cashew korma ⓥ

An electric coffee grinder is inexpensive and is invaluable for turning nuts into powder in an instant, and also for grinding spices—it's one of my favorite pieces of equipment.

SERVES 4
PREPARATION 20 MINUTES
COOKING 40 MINUTES

1 tablespoon canola oil
1 large onion, finely chopped
2 garlic cloves, crushed
1 teaspoon turmeric
1 tablespoon ground cumin
1 tablespoon ground coriander
½ cup cashew nuts
1¾ cups coconut milk
1¾ cups water
small handful of fresh curry leaves
   (optional)
6 oz okra, trimmed
2 cups cauliflower florets
3½ cups broccoli florets
salt and black pepper
chopped cilantro leaves, to garnish
basmati rice or other long-grain rice,
   to serve

1 Heat the canola oil in a large saucepan, add the onion, cover, and cook for about 10 minutes, or until tender. Stir in the garlic, turmeric, cumin, and ground coriander, and cook for a minute or two longer.

2 Grind the cashews to a powder in a coffee grinder, food processor, or using the fine grater in a hand mill. Add them to the pan, along with the coconut milk.

3 For a really smooth sauce, you can now puree the whole lot in a food processor or blender (or use an immersion blender in the saucepan) or, if you prefer some texture, leave it as it is.

4 Return the mixture to the pan, if you've pureed it, and add the water and curry leaves, if using. Let simmer for 20–30 minutes, stirring from time to time, until thickened.

5 Just before the sauce is ready, bring a 2 inch depth of water to a boil in a large saucepan. Add the okra, cauliflower, and broccoli, bring back to a boil, cover, and cook for about 6 minutes, or until tender. Drain, then add the vegetables to the korma, stirring gently. Season with salt and black pepper.

6 You can serve this at once, but if there's time, let it rest for a while—even overnight—for the flavors to intensify. Then gently reheat. Sprinkle with cilantro before serving and serve with hot white basmati rice.

Oven-baked ratatouille with balsamic vinegar & caper berries ⓥ

SERVES 4
PREPARATION 10 MINUTES
COOKING 40 MINUTES

2 red onions, each sliced into 6 or 8
1 large zucchini, cut into
    ½ inch pieces
1 large eggplant, cut into
    ½ inch pieces
2 red bell peppers, cored, seeded, and
    cut into ½ inch pieces
2 tablespoons olive oil
1–2 tablespoons balsamic vinegar
1 (14½ oz) can diced tomatoes
4 garlic cloves, coarsely chopped
1–2 tablespoons caper berries, drained
salt and black pepper

1 Put the onions, zucchini, eggplant, and red bell peppers into a roasting pan with the olive oil and 1 tablespoon of the balsamic vinegar. Toss the vegetables to coat them all with the oil and vinegar, then season with salt and black pepper.

2 Bake in a preheated oven, at 400°F, uncovered, for 20 minutes, then add the tomatoes, garlic, and caper berries. Stir well and cook for another 20 minutes, or until all the vegetables are tender.

3 Taste the ratatouille and add a little more balsamic vinegar and salt and black pepper, if necessary. Serve hot, warm, or cold.

Lentil casserole with mashed potatoes

This is such a tasty, satisfying dish and I find it goes well with even the most hardened carnivores. It's convenient, too, because it can be made in advance, ready for the final cooking.

SERVES 4
PREPARATION 30 MINUTES
COOKING 1 HOUR

9 russet or Yukon gold potatoes
   (about 2¼ lb), peeled and cut
   into even pieces
2 tablespoons olive oil
2 large onions, chopped
2 garlic cloves, crushed
1 (14½ oz) can diced tomatoes
1 (15 oz) can green lentils, drained,
   or 2 cups cooked green lentils
⅓ cup chopped sun-dried tomatoes
1 tablespoon ketchup
1 tablespoon butter
2 cups shredded cheddar cheese
salt and black pepper
cooked green peas or kale, to serve

1 Put the potatoes into a saucepan, cover with water, and bring to a boil. Boil for about 20 minutes, or until tender.

2 Meanwhile, heat the olive oil in a large saucepan, add the onions, cover, and cook for 15 minutes, or until tender, lightly browned, and sweet. Remove from the heat and add the garlic, tomatoes, lentils, sun-dried tomatoes, and ketchup. Season with salt and black pepper to taste.

3 Drain the boiled potatoes, reserving the water, then mash with the butter and enough of the reserved water to make a creamy consistency. Stir in two-thirds of the cheese.

4 Pour the lentil mixture into a shallow casserole dish and spread the potato on top. Sprinkle with the remaining cheese and bake in a preheated oven, at 400°F, for 40 minutes, until golden brown. Serve with peas or kale.

Kedgeree with eggs & tarragon butter

SERVES 4
PREPARATION 20 MINUTES
COOKING 35 MINUTES

1 tablespoon olive oil
1 large onion, chopped
3 garlic cloves, finely chopped
¼ teaspoon turmeric
1½ cups basmati rice
¾ cup split red lentils
3 cups water
2 tablespoons lemon juice
4–6 hen eggs or 8–12 quail eggs,
    hard-boiled and halved
salad of peppery greens, such
    as arugula, to serve
salt and black pepper

FOR THE TARRAGON BUTTER

6 tablespoons butter, softened
¼ cup chopped tarragon

1 Heat the olive oil in a large, heavy saucepan, add the onion, cover, and cook gently for 10 minutes, stirring from time to time.

2 Stir in the garlic and turmeric and cook for a minute or two longer, then add the rice and lentils and stir until they are coated with the onion and spice mixture.

3 Pour in the water and bring to a boil, then reduce the heat, cover, and let cook gently for 20 minutes, until the lentils are pale, the rice is tender, and all the water has been absorbed.

4 While the rice is cooking, make the tarragon butter. Beat the butter with a fork until creamy, then stir in the tarragon. Form into a log shape on a piece of wax paper or aluminum foil and refrigerate until required.

5 Using a fork, gently stir the lemon juice into the rice—this will brighten the color instantly—and season with salt and black pepper. Turn the mixture into a warmed shallow serving dish or onto individual plates and top with pieces of tarragon butter and the cooked eggs. Serve at once with a salad of peppery greens, such as arugula.

Green risotto with spinach, peas, herbs & green beans •ⱽ

It's hard to believe that such a delectable risotto is actually low in fat and is still such a treat. If you want to serve an accompaniment, roasted tomatoes complement it perfectly.

SERVES 4
PREPARATION 30 MINUTES, PLUS
    STANDING
COOKING 35 MINUTES

1 tablespoon olive oil
1 onion, chopped
1 celery stick, finely chopped
1¼ cups 1 inch green bean pieces
1 teaspoon vegetable stock powder
    or 1 vegetable bouillon cube
1 large garlic clove, crushed
2 cups risotto rice
1 cup white wine
4 cups baby leaf spinach
1 cup fresh or frozen green peas
3–4 tablespoons chopped herbs—
    parsley, mint, dill, chives, whatever
    is available
salt and black pepper
grated or shaved Parmesan-style
    cheese, to serve (optional)

1 Heat the olive oil in a large saucepan, add the onion and celery, and stir, then cover and cook for 7 minutes.

2 Meanwhile, cook the green beans in a saucepan of boiling water for 4–5 minutes, or until just tender. Drain and set aside, reserving the liquid. Make the liquid up to 5 cups and put into a saucepan with the vegetable stock powder or bouillon cube. Bring to a boil, then reduce the heat and keep the stock hot over gentle heat.

3 Add the garlic and rice to the onion and celery in the pan and stir well. Add half the white wine and continue cooking, stirring all the time, until the wine has simmered away. Repeat the process with the remaining wine, then add the hot stock in the same way, a ladleful at a time.

4 When the rice is tender and all or most of the stock has been used—after about 25 minutes—add the spinach, reserved beans, peas, and herbs, cover, and let stand for 5 minutes, until the spinach is cooked.

5 Season with salt and black pepper and serve at once with a little Parmesan, if desired.

Tagliatelle of cabbage with cream cheese, herb & garlic sauce

SERVES 4

PREPARATION 10 MINUTES

COOKING 10 MINUTES

2 lb hearty pale green cabbage,
 hard core removed and leaves
 cut into long strands like tagliatelle
1 cup low-fat cream cheese
2 garlic cloves, crushed
¼ cup chopped parsley and chives
grated zest of 1 lemon
salt and black pepper
shaved or grated Parmesan-style
 cheese, to serve (optional)

1 Fill a large saucepan halfway with water and bring to a boil. Add the cabbage, bring back to a boil, and cook, uncovered, for 5–6 minutes, or until tender. Drain and return the cabbage to the saucepan.

2 Add the cream cheese to the pan, along with the garlic, herbs, lemon zest, and some salt and black pepper to taste. Mix well gently, then serve on warmed plates topped with a little Parmesan, if you desire.

Mediterranean stuffed red peppers with mashed cauliflower

The mashed cauliflower is like a light version of mashed potatoes but with a fraction of the calories. It's also low in carbs and a good way of getting one of the daily "five portions" of fruit and vegetables—cauliflower counts as a portion but potatoes don't. You could also serve these stuffed red peppers with cauliflower "rice" (see page 108).

SERVES 4
PREPARATION 10 MINUTES
COOKING 30 MINUTES

4 red bell peppers
7 oz feta cheese, cut into ½ inch cubes
8 teaspoons pesto
16 cherry tomatoes, halved

FOR THE MASHED CAULIFLOWER

1 cauliflower, trimmed and cut into florets
2 tablespoons butter
salt and black pepper

1 Halve the bell peppers, cutting right through the stems, too, if you can. Trim the insides and rinse away all the seeds. Put the bell peppers in a roasting pan or large shallow casserole dish. Divide the feta among the peppers, then spoon 2 teaspoons of the pesto over the cheese in each bell pepper. Finally, top with the tomatoes, skin side up.

2 Bake in a preheated oven, at 400°F, for 30 minutes, or until the tops are charring and the insides full of luscious juice.

3 Meanwhile, make the mashed cauliflower. Bring a 2 inch depth of water to a boil in a large saucepan. Add the cauliflower, bring back to a boil, cover, and cook for 5–6 minutes, until tender. Drain well. Put the cauliflower into a food processor with the butter and some salt and black pepper and process to a smooth, thick mixture. Return to the saucepan and gently reheat, stirring so that it doesn't catch, then serve with the stuffed red peppers.

Laksa ⱽ

You need Thai paste for this Malaysian soup/stew—most contain shrimp paste so read the label to find one that's vegetarian.

SERVES 4
PREPARATION 15 MINUTES
COOKING 20 MINUTES

4 oz rice noodles
2 tablespoons sesame oil
1 tablespoon vegetarian Thai paste
8 oz shiitake mushrooms, sliced
1 red chile, seeded and sliced
1¾ cups coconut milk
2½ cups water
1 eggplant, stem trimmed
2 bok choy, trimmed and halved
12 baby corn, halved diagonally
salt and black pepper
1 cup coarsely chopped cilantro,
  to garnish

1 Put the noodles into a bowl, cover with boiling water, and let soak for 5–10 minutes, or according to the package directions, until tender, then drain.

2 Heat 1 tablespoon of the sesame oil in a large saucepan, add the Thai paste, and let it sizzle for a few seconds until aromatic, then stir in the mushrooms and chile. Pour in the coconut milk and water, then reduce the heat, cover, and let simmer for 10–15 minutes.

3 Meanwhile, cut the eggplant into ¼ inch-thick slices and brush on both sides with the remaining oil. Place in a broiler pan and cook under a preheated broiler for about 7 minutes on each side, until tender and lightly browned. Let cool, then cut into dice.

4 Cook the bok choy in a saucepan of boiling water for about 6 minutes, or until tender. Drain well.

5 Add the noodles, eggplant, bok choy, and corn to the coconut mixture. Bring to a boil and simmer gently for a minute or two to heat everything through and cook the corn.

6 Season with salt and black pepper as necessary, ladle into warmed bowls, and top each with some cilantro to garnish.

Stir-fry with sizzling tofu ⓥ

A fine microplane grater revolutionizes garlic crushing; just grate the garlic, skin and all, for perfect results. (It also works for fresh ginger root—there is no need to peel it first.) Immerse the grater in water immediately after use to make cleaning easier.

SERVES 6
PREPARATION 15 MINUTES,
   PLUS MARINATING
COOKING 15 MINUTES

1 tablespoon sesame oil
2 teaspoons vegetarian Thai red
   curry paste
2 garlic cloves, crushed
2 teaspoons grated fresh ginger root
3 cups bean sprouts
1 red bell pepper, cored, seeded, and
   thinly sliced
bunch of scallions, trimmed
   and chopped
2 cups button mushrooms
2 cups snow peas (halved lengthwise)
1 tablespoon soy sauce
cilantro leaves, to garnish
salt

FOR THE TOFU

1 tablespoon grated fresh ginger root
4 garlic cloves, crushed
1 teaspoon packed brown sugar
1 teaspoon Dijon mustard
¼ cup soy sauce
1 lb firm tofu, drained and cut
   into ¼ inch slices
light olive oil, for pan-frying

1 Start with the tofu. Put the ginger, garlic, sugar, mustard, and soy sauce into a shallow dish and mix together. Toss the pieces of tofu in the mixture until they are well coated. Let marinate for as long as you can—10–30 minutes or up to 24 hours.

2 To make the stir-fry, heat the sesame oil in a wok until smoking hot. Add the curry paste and stir for a few seconds over the heat, then add the garlic and ginger and stir again. Add all the vegetables to the wok and stir-fry for 1–2 minutes, then cover and let cook for 5 minutes, or until the vegetables are tender. Stir in the soy sauce.

3 Meanwhile, drain the tofu, saving any remaining marinade. Heat a little olive oil in a skillet and cook the tofu on both sides. You will probably have to cook in 2 batches, so keep the first batch hot under a preheated broiler.

4 Add any reserved marinade to the vegetables. Check the seasoning and add some salt, if necessary, then serve with the sizzling hot tofu and garnish with cilantro.

Three-bean chili with multicolor peppers ⓥ

SERVES 4

PREPARATION 20 MINUTES

COOKING 30–35 MINUTES

1 tablespoon olive oil

1 onion, chopped

2 garlic cloves, finely chopped

1 green chile, seeded and chopped

1 red, 1 yellow, and 1 green bell
   pepper, all cored, seeded, and
   chopped

1 (15 oz) can cranberry beans

1 (15 oz) can red kidney beans

1 (15 oz) can pinto beans

1 (14½ oz) can diced tomatoes

salt and black pepper

Tabasco, to taste (optional)

1 Heat the olive oil in a large saucepan, add the onion, cover, and sauté without browning for 5 minutes. Add the garlic, chile, and bell peppers, stir, then cover and sauté for another 15–20 minutes, or until the bell peppers are tender.

2 Add all the beans, together with their liquid, and the tomatoes. Stir and bring to a simmer, then cook over gentle heat for about 10 minutes, until the vegetables are tender.

3 Taste and season with salt and black pepper as necessary, and a dash of Tabasco if you think it needs to be a little hotter, then serve.

Spaghetti with black olive & tomato sauce ⱱ

SERVES 4
PREPARATION 15 MINUTES
COOKING 30 MINUTES

2 tablespoons olive oil
1 onion, finely chopped
2 garlic cloves, chopped
2 (14½ oz) cans diced tomatoes
1 cup red wine
1 lb spaghetti
½–1 cup pitted and coarsely chopped
   ripe Kalamata olives
salt and black pepper
Parmesan-style cheese shavings,
   to serve (optional)

1 Heat 1 tablespoon of the olive oil in a large, heavy saucepan, add the onion, cover, and cook gently for 10 minutes, stirring from time to time. Stir in the garlic and cook for a minute or two longer.

2 Add the tomatoes and wine to the pan. Bring to a boil and let boil, uncovered, stirring from time to time, for 20 minutes or until thick.

3 Meanwhile, bring a large saucepan of water to a boil for the pasta. When it comes to a rolling boil, add the spaghetti and cook according to the package directions.

4 Liquidize the sauce in a food processor or blender, or using an immersion blender, and return it to the saucepan. Stir in the olives, season with salt and black pepper, and reheat.

5 Drain the spaghetti, return to the pan with the remaining olive oil, and toss gently. Then either add the sauce and toss with the spaghetti, or serve the spaghetti on warmed plates and spoon the tomato and olive sauce on top. Hand around the Parmesan separately, if using.

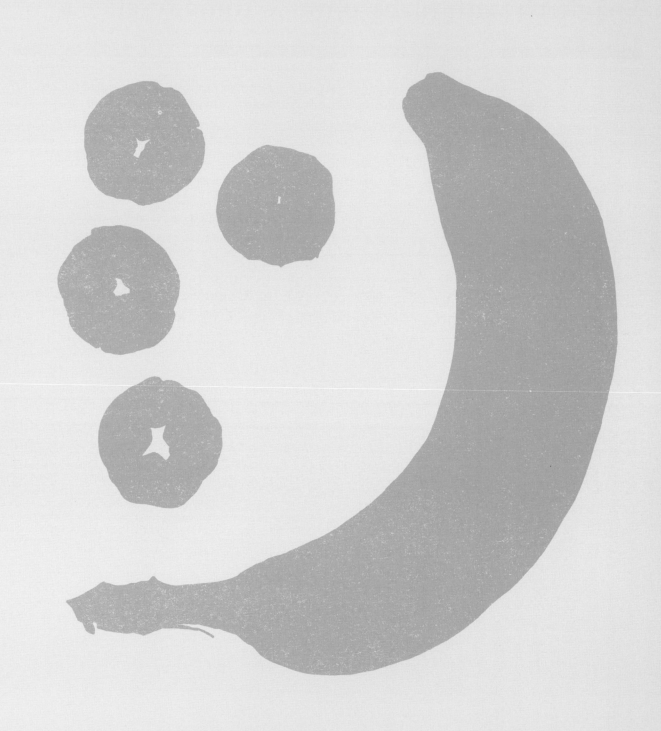

Midweek meals

Chargrilled artichoke heart & basil frittata

If you can't get chargrilled artichoke hearts, any halved artichoke hearts in oil from a jar or loose from a deli will be fine. Any leftover frittata is wonderful cold, perhaps served with a lemon mayonnaise and a crisp green salad.

SERVES 4
PREPARATION 10 MINUTES
COOKING 15 MINUTES

8 chargrilled halved artichoke hearts
  in oil
2 cups shredded vegetarian Gruyère
  cheese or similar cheese, such as
  Swiss or Gouda
8 eggs, whisked
salt and black pepper
handful of basil, coarsely chopped
leafy salad with vinaigrette dressing
  (see page 66), to serve

1 Drain the artichoke hearts but save the oil. Heat 2 tablespoons of the oil in an 11 inch skillet or in a gratin dish that will go under the broiler.

2 Arrange the artichoke hearts in a single layer on the bottom of the pan or dish, sprinkle with half the cheese, then pour the eggs evenly over the top. Season with salt and black pepper and top with the basil and the remaining cheese.

3 Set the pan over moderate heat, cover with a lid or a plate, and cook for about 5 minutes, or until the bottom is set and getting browned.

4 Remove the covering from the pan and put the pan under a preheated hot broiler for about 10 minutes, or until the frittata has puffed up and browned, and is set in the center. Serve at once with a leafy salad dressed with vinaigrette.

Spicy okra with red onions, mustard seeds & brown rice •

SERVES 4
PREPARATION 20 MINUTES
COOKING 25–30 MINUTES

1 tablespoon olive oil
2 red onions, sliced
4 garlic cloves, chopped
4 teaspoons ground coriander
½ teaspoon turmeric
1 teaspoon mustard seeds
1 lb okra, trimmed and cut
   into 1 inch pieces
1 (14½ oz) can diced tomatoes
½ teaspoon garam masala
sugar, to taste
salt and black pepper
cilantro leaves, to garnish

FOR THE RICE

1¼ cups brown long-grain rice
2½ cups water

1 Put the rice into a heavy saucepan with the water. Bring to a boil, then cover, reduce the heat, and cook over low heat for 20 minutes, or according to the package directions, until the rice is tender and all the water has been absorbed. Remove from the heat and let stand, still covered, until you're ready to serve.

2 Meanwhile, to make the spicy okra, heat the olive oil in a large saucepan, add the onions, cover, and sauté for 10–15 minutes, until tender. Add the garlic, ground coriander, turmeric, and mustard seeds and stir over the heat for a few seconds until they smell aromatic.

3 Add the okra and stir to coat with the onion and spice mixture, then add the tomatoes. Cover and let cook gently for 15–20 minutes, or until the okra is tender.

4 Stir in the garam masala, taste, and season with salt, black pepper, and a dash of sugar, if necessary. Sprinkle with fresh cilantro and serve with the rice.

Creamy three-cheese cauliflower with walnuts

SERVES 4
PREPARATION 15 MINUTES
COOKING 20 MINUTES

1 cauliflower, trimmed and cut into
  ½ inch pieces
1¼ cups cream cheese
1 teaspoon Dijon mustard
1 cup crumbled blue cheese
¼ cup coarsely chopped walnuts
½ cup shredded cheddar cheese
salt and black pepper
peppery greens, to serve

1 Bring a 2 inch depth of water to a boil in a saucepan. Add the cauliflower, bring back to a boil, and cook for about 8 minutes, or until tender. Drain, then return the cauliflower to the pan.

2 Mix the cream cheese and mustard with the cauliflower, then stir in the blue cheese. Season with a little salt, if necessary, and plenty of black pepper.

3 Pour the mixture into a shallow gratin dish. Sprinkle the walnuts on top, then cover with the cheddar (this helps to prevent the walnuts from burning). Cook under a preheated hot broiler for 10–15 minutes, or until the top is golden brown and the inside hot and bubbling. Serve at once with peppery greens.

Chunky lentil, onion & chestnut loaf with sherry gravy •

SERVES 4
PREPARATION 20 MINUTES
COOKING 1 HOUR 20 MINUTES

⅔ cup dried split red lentils
1¼ cups water
1 bay leaf
1 teaspoon olive oil
1 onion, chopped
3 garlic cloves, chopped
1 celery stick, chopped
2 tomatoes, chopped
18 vacuum-packed or canned
    whole peeled chestnuts, drained
    if necessary, coarsely chopped
1 teaspoon soy sauce
salt and black pepper

FOR THE GRAVY

2½ cups water
1 tablespoon vegetarian stock powder
3 tablespoons soy sauce
1½ tablespoons red currant jelly or
    cranberry preserves
1 tablespoon cornstarch
1½ tablespoons orange juice
1½ tablespoons sherry

1 Line an 8½ x 4½ x 2½ inch loaf pan with a strip of nonstick parchment paper to cover the bottom and narrow sides.

2 Put the red lentils into a saucepan with the water and bay leaf. Bring to a boil, then reduce the heat and let simmer gently for 15–20 minutes, or according to the package directions, until the lentils are tender and all the water has been absorbed.

3 Meanwhile, heat the olive oil in a skillet, add the onion, and sauté for 10 minutes, stirring often to prevent it from sticking. Remove from the heat and add to the lentils, along with the garlic, celery, tomatoes, chestnuts, soy sauce, and some salt and black pepper.

4 Spoon the lentil mixture into the prepared loaf pan, press down well, and smooth the surface. Bake in a preheated oven, at 400°F, for 1 hour, until firm.

5 Meanwhile, make the gravy. Put the water, stock powder, soy sauce, and red currant jelly or cranberry preserves into a saucepan and bring to a boil. Blend the cornstarch with the orange juice and sherry. Stir a little of the hot liquid into the cornstarch mixture, then add to the saucepan. Stir well, then simmer over gentle heat until slightly thickened and season to taste with salt and black pepper.

6 Loosen the edges of the lentil loaf by slipping a knife down the sides, then invert the pan over a plate and turn out the loaf. Serve in thick slices, with the gravy.

Coulibiac with sour cream sauce

This makes a great spring or summer meal, served with baby new potatoes and buttered baby beans or zucchini. For a special occasion it's also nice served with hollandaise sauce (see page 132).

SERVES 4
PREPARATION 20 MINUTES
COOKING 55 MINUTES

⅔ cup basmati rice or other long-grain rice
1 tablespoon olive oil
2 tablespoons butter
1 large onion, finely chopped
2 cups shredded green cabbage
4 cups baby button mushrooms
3 hard-boiled eggs, coarsely chopped
¼ cup chopped dill
2 sheets of ready-to-bake puff pastry
beaten egg, to glaze
sea salt flakes, for sprinkling
salt and black pepper

FOR THE SAUCE
¼ cup chopped chives
1¼ cups sour cream

1 Bring a saucepan of water to a boil. Add the rice, bring back to a boil, and boil for about 10 minutes, or according to the package directions, until tender, then drain and set aside.

2 Meanwhile, heat the olive oil and butter in a large saucepan, add the onion, cover, and cook for 5 minutes. Add the cabbage and mushrooms, stir, cover, and cook for about 10 minutes, or until the cabbage is tender. Remove from the heat.

3 Add the drained rice, the eggs, and dill to the onion mixture and season with salt and black pepper. Let cool a little.

4 Put the puff pastry sheets side by side on a large baking sheet and press them lightly together where they meet to make one large piece. Trim 1½ inches off the sides of the pastry.

5 Spoon the rice mixture along the center of the piece of pastry, on top of the seam. Make diagonal cuts in the pastry on each side of the rice filling and fold them alternately over the filling to create a braided effect; trim off any excess pastry. Brush with beaten egg and sprinkle with the sea salt. Bake in a preheated oven, at 400°F, for 40 minutes, or until the coulibiac is puffy and golden brown.

6 To make the sauce, stir the chives into the sour cream and season with salt and black pepper. Serve with the coulibiac.

Eggs in coconut curry sauce with cauliflower "rice"

SERVES 4
PREPARATION 20 MINUTES
COOKING 15 MINUTES

1 tablespoon olive oil
1 small onion, finely chopped
1 small green chile, seeded and
  sliced
2 garlic cloves, crushed
2 teaspoons grated fresh ginger root
2 tomatoes, chopped
2 teaspoons coriander seeds
4 cardamom pods
1¾ cups coconut milk
3 tablespoons chopped cilantro,
  plus extra to garnish
8 hard-boiled eggs, halved

FOR THE CAULIFLOWER "RICE"

1 cauliflower, trimmed and cut
  into florets
salt and black pepper

1 Heat the olive oil in a saucepan, add the onion, cover, and cook for 5 minutes. Stir in the chile, garlic, ginger, and tomatoes. Stir and cook for another 2–3 minutes.

2 Meanwhile, crush the coriander seeds and cardamom pods, using a coffee grinder or mortar and pestle, and add to the onion mixture. Stir for a few seconds, then add the coconut milk and cook over gentle heat for another 2–3 minutes. Stir in the cilantro and season with salt and black pepper.

3 Gently put the hard-boiled eggs into the coconut mixture, spooning it over them, and leave, covered, over gentle heat for the flavors to steep while you deal with the cauliflower.

4 Bring a 2 inch depth of water to a boil in a large saucepan. Add the cauliflower, bring back to a boil, cover, and cook for 4 minutes, until just tender. Drain well.

5 Put the cauliflower into a food processor with some salt and black pepper and process to a grainy texture—like cooked rice—but stop before it turns to mash. Return it to the saucepan and gently reheat, stirring so that it doesn't catch. Garnish the egg curry with the remaining cilantro and serve with the cauliflower "rice."

Sweet potato & coconut dhal with cilantro ⓥ

This is delicious—and tastes even better the next day. Note that the spices are added after the lentils are tender—if you add them at the beginning, they can prevent the lentils from becoming tender, as can tomatoes or anything acidic.

SERVES 4
PREPARATION 15 MINUTES
COOKING 20 MINUTES

3 orange-fleshed sweet potatoes,
 peeled and cut into ½ inch cubes
1 cup dried split red lentils
1 green chile, seeded and sliced
1¾ cups coconut milk
2 cups water
1 teaspoon grated fresh ginger root
1 teaspoon ground cinnamon
½ teaspoon turmeric
salt and black pepper
chopped cilantro, to garnish
cabbage, rice, or cauliflower "rice"
 (see page 108), to serve

1 Put the sweet potatoes into a saucepan with the lentils, chile, coconut milk, and water. Bring to a boil, then reduce the heat and let cook gently, uncovered, for 15–20 minutes, until the sweet potato and lentils are tender and the mixture looks thick.

2 Stir in the ginger, cinnamon, turmeric, and some salt and black pepper to taste, then cook gently for a few more minutes to blend in the flavors. Sprinkle with cilantro and serve with some lightly cooked cabbage, plain-cooked rice, or cauliflower "rice."

Banana curry with cashew rice ⓥ

I love this gentle, sweet curry and it's so quick to make. You could use 2–3 plantains in place of the bananas, if you prefer, but cook them for a few minutes longer.

SERVES 4
PREPARATION 25 MINUTES
COOKING 30 MINUTES

1 lb new potatoes, halved
2 tablespoons olive oil
1 onion, chopped
2 green bell peppers, cored, seeded, and chopped
2 teaspoons mustard seeds
½ teaspoon turmeric
1 tablespoon grated fresh ginger root
4 garlic cloves, crushed
⅔ cup dried curry leaves
4 large underripe bananas, sliced
1¼ cups water
2 x 4 inch fresh pieces of coconut, chopped, or 1 cup shredded dried coconut
4 teaspoons fresh, strained and seeded tamarind (from a jar)
salt and black pepper
1 heaping tablespoon coarsely chopped cilantro, to garnish

FOR THE RICE

1 cup basmati rice or other long-grain rice
1 cup roasted cashew nuts, chopped

1 Start by cooking the rice. Bring a large saucepan of water to a boil, add the rice, bring back to a boil, then reduce the heat and let simmer for 15–20 minutes, or until the rice is just tender. Drain, rinse with boiling water, drain again well, then return it to the saucepan and keep warm over gentle heat until required.

2 To make the curry, put the potatoes into a saucepan, cover with water, and bring to a boil, then reduce the heat and simmer for 10–15 minutes, until just tender, then drain.

3 Meanwhile, heat the olive oil in a large, heavy saucepan, add the onion and bell peppers, cover, and cook gently for 10 minutes, stirring from time to time.

4 Add the mustard seeds, stirring over the heat for a minute or two until they start to pop, then stir in the turmeric, ginger, garlic, and curry leaves and cook for a minute or two longer.

5 Stir in the drained potatoes and the bananas, then add the water, coconut, and tamarind paste. Bring to a boil, then reduce the heat and let cook gently for 5–10 minutes, until the sauce is thick and the flavors blended. Season with salt and black pepper.

6 Quickly add the cashews to the rice and fork through, then serve the rice and curry together on warmed plates and garnish with cilantro.

Chickpea stew with fruity couscous ⓥ

SERVES 4
PREPARATION 15 MINUTES
COOKING 30 MINUTES

2 tablespoons olive oil
2 onions, chopped
2 garlic cloves, crushed
1 teaspoon ground ginger
1 teaspoon turmeric
½ teaspoon saffron threads
2 fennel bulbs, trimmed and quartered
1 zucchini, cut into sticks
1 small eggplant, cut into ½ inch dice
1 (14½ oz) can tomatoes
1 (15 oz) can chickpeas, drained
1¼–2½ cups pitted green olives
1 preserved lemon, rinsed in cold
    water and chopped, or 1 thin-
    skinned lemon, finely sliced
1¼ cups vegetable stock
salt and black pepper
1 heaping tablespoon coarsely chopped
    cilantro, to garnish

FOR THE FRUITY COUSCOUS

2 cups couscous
1 tablespoon olive oil
2 cups water
⅓ cup golden raisins
½ cup chopped dried apricots

1 Heat the olive oil in a large, heavy saucepan, add the onions, cover, and cook gently for 10 minutes, stirring from time to time. Stir in the garlic and cook for a minute or two longer.

2 Add the ginger, turmeric, and saffron to the pan and stir, then add the fennel, zucchini, and eggplant. Stir for a minute or two, then add the tomatoes, chickpeas, olives, lemon, and stock. Bring to a boil, then reduce the heat, cover, and let simmer for about 15 minutes, or until the vegetables are tender. Season with salt and black pepper.

3 While the stew is cooking, put the couscous into a saucepan with the olive oil, water, golden raisins, and apricots and bring to a boil. Cover and simmer for 5 minutes, then remove from the heat and let stand, covered, until required. Fluff with a fork, serve with the stew (which is an Moroccan-inspired "tagine") and garnish with cilantro.

Cornmeal with leeks & blue cheese

SERVES 4
PREPARATION 15 MINUTES
COOKING 20–40 MINUTES

6 leeks, trimmed and sliced into
  2 inch lengths
2 cups instant polenta or 1 cup
  regular cornmeal
8 oz blue cheese, broken into pieces
salt and black pepper
good-quality olive oil (optional)
  and coarsely ground black pepper,
  to serve

1 Fill a saucepan with water and bring to a boil. Add the leeks, bring back to a boil, cover, and cook for 8–10 minutes, or until the leeks are tender. Drain, reserving the water, and keep the leeks warm.

2 For instant polenta, measure the cooking water and make up to 3¾ cups with more water, if necessary. Put this liquid into a large saucepan and heat to a boil. Sprinkle the polenta on top in a steady stream, stirring all the time with a wooden spoon. Cook according to the package directions, until thick and soft, then remove from the heat. If using regular cornmeal, bring 4 cups water to a boil, add the cornmeal, and cook according to the package directions, stirring every few minutes to prevent lumps from forming

3 Add the leeks, blue cheese, and a seasoning of salt and black pepper (remembering that the cheese is salty) to the cornmeal/polenta and stir gently to distribute the leeks and cheese through the mixture. Serve on warmed plates, swirl with a little olive oil if using, and grind some coarse black pepper over the top.

Sesame-roasted tofu with satay sauce & broccoli •

SERVES 4
PREPARATION 20 MINUTES
COOKING 20 MINUTES

1 lb firm tofu, drained
¼ cup soy sauce
2 tablespoons toasted sesame oil
2 tablespoons sesame seeds
1 large head of broccoli, trimmed
   and broken into florets

FOR THE SATAY SAUCE

¼ cup peanut butter (plain or chunky)
1¾ cups coconut milk (see page 70)
2 garlic cloves, crushed
2 teaspoons grated fresh ginger root
¼–½ teaspoon dried red pepper flakes
2–3 teaspoons packed brown sugar
¼ cup chopped cilantro, to garnish

1   Blot the tofu dry on paper towels and cut into thin strips about ¼ inch thick. Put the strips on a plate in a single layer, pour the soy sauce on top, then turn the strips so that they are all coated.

2   Heat the sesame oil in a broiler pan or shallow roasting pan under a preheated hot broiler. Put the tofu strips in the pan in a single layer and sprinkle with half the sesame seeds, then immediately turn them over and coat with the remaining sesame seeds.

3   Put the pan back under the broiler and cook for about 10 minutes, or until the tofu is crisp and browned, then turn the pieces over and broil the other side.

4   Meanwhile, make the satay sauce. Put the peanut butter into a saucepan and gradually stir in the coconut milk to make a smooth sauce, then add the garlic, ginger, and red pepper flakes. Heat gently, taste, and add sugar to taste. Remove from the heat and set aside until required.

5   About 5–10 minutes before the tofu is ready, bring a ½ inch depth of water to a boil in a large saucepan. Add the broccoli, bring back to a boil, cover, and cook for 4–5 minutes, or until just tender. Drain.

6   Put some broccoli, tofu, and a serving of satay sauce on each plate, sprinkle the sauce with some cilantro, and serve.

Indonesian savory stuffed pineapples ⓥ

Ketjap manis is an Indonesian soy sauce that is sweeter and less salty than other types. If you can't get it, just use normal soy sauce and a teaspoon of brown sugar or a dash of honey.

SERVES 4
PREPARATION 20 MINUTES
COOKING 45 MINUTES

1½ cups basmati rice or other
   long-grain rice
2½ cups water
2 small pineapples with leafy tops
1 tablespoon sesame oil
1 onion, chopped
1 cup whole cashew nuts,
   toasted under the broiler
1 cup frozen peas, thawed
2–4 tablespoons ketjap manis
   (see above)
2 teaspoons packed brown sugar
3 tablespoons dried coconut,
   toasted under the broiler

1 Put the rice into a saucepan with the water. Bring to a boil, then cover, reduce the heat, and let cook gently for 15 minutes, or according to the package directions, until the rice is tender and all the water has been absorbed.

2 Halve the pineapples lengthwise, cutting right down through the leaves. Cut around the inside edge of the pineapple about ¼ inch away from the skin and scoop out the flesh. Discard the hard core. Chop the flesh into ¼ inch pieces.

3 Heat the sesame oil in a saucepan, add the onion, cover, and cook gently for 10 minutes, until tender. Remove from the heat and stir in ¼ cup of the cooked rice together with the pineapple flesh, cashew nuts, peas, ketjap manis, and sugar. Taste and add a little more ketjap manis, if necessary.

4 Pile the cashew mixture into the pineapple shells, piling them up well and sprinkle the tops with the dried coconut. Put the stuffed pineapples into a shallow casserole dish or roasting pan and cover with aluminum foil. Bake in a preheated oven, at 350°F, for 30 minutes. After 20 minutes, put the remaining rice in a casserole dish, cover, and place in the oven to reheat. Serve immediately.

Corn fritters with tomato sauce

SERVES 4
PREPARATION 15 MINUTES
COOKING 15 MINUTES

1⅔ cups corn kernels, freshly cut
 from the cob, frozen, or drained
 unsweetened canned kernels
1 egg, separated
3 tablespoons whole-wheat flour
canola oil, for pan-frying
salt and black pepper

FOR THE TOMATO SAUCE

1 tablespoon olive oil
1 onion, finely chopped
2 garlic cloves, chopped
1 (14½ oz) can diced tomatoes

1 First make the tomato sauce. Heat the olive oil in a saucepan, add the onion, and sauté for 7–10 minutes, until tender. Stir in the garlic, then add the tomatoes and simmer for about 15 minutes, or until all the extra liquid has gone. For a smoother texture, puree in a food processor or blender. Season with salt and black pepper and set aside.

2 To make the fritters, put the corn kernels into a bowl with the egg yolk, whole-wheat flour, and some salt and black pepper and mix well. Whisk the egg white in a clean, grease-proof bowl until it stands in stiff peaks, then gently fold into the corn kernels mixture.

3 Heat a little canola oil in a skillet, then drop tablespoons of the corn kernels mixture into the oil and cook on both sides until crisp. Drain on paper towels. Keep the first batch warm under a preheated broiler or in a cool oven while you cook the rest, then serve with the tomato sauce.

Tagliatelle with creamy spinach & nutmeg sauce

SERVES 4
PREPARATION 15 MINUTES
COOKING 20 MINUTES

1 lb tagliatelle
1 lb spinach leaves
2 tablespoons butter
2 tablespoons olive oil
1 onion, finely chopped
2 garlic cloves, chopped
2 teaspoons cornstarch
1¼ cups light cream or heavy cream
grated nutmeg
salt and black pepper
grated Parmesan-style cheese,
    to serve (optional)

1 Bring a large saucepan of water to a boil for the pasta. When it comes to a boil, add the tagliatelle and cook according to the package directions.

2 Meanwhile, wash the spinach, then place in a large saucepan with just the water clinging to the leaves and cook over high heat for 3–4 minutes, or until tender. Drain thoroughly, reserving the water, and set the spinach aside. Make the water up to ⅔ cup.

3 Heat the butter and 1 tablespoon of the olive oil in a large, heavy saucepan, add the onion, cover, and cook gently for 10 minutes, stirring from time to time. Stir in the garlic and cook for a minute or two longer.

4 Stir the cornstarch into the saucepan, then add the spinach water and stir over the heat for a minute or two until thickened. Add the spinach and the cream, then grate in a good flavoring of nutmeg and season with salt and black pepper.

5 Drain the tagliatelle and return to the pan with the remaining olive oil and toss gently. Then either add the sauce and toss with the pasta, or serve the pasta on warmed plates and spoon the spinach sauce on top. Hand around the Parmesan separately, if using.

Rosti with applesauce ⓥ

I love this combination: crisp, an irresistible Swiss-style rosti—like a large hash brown—with a sweet applesauce. A salad of sliced cabbage and grated carrot tossed in vinaigrette goes well with it.

SERVES 4
PREPARATION 15 MINUTES
COOKING 20 MINUTES

9 russet or Yukon gold potatoes,
    scrubbed but not peeled
1 small onion
1 tablespoon chopped rosemary
¼ cup olive oil
salt and black pepper
rosemary sprigs, to garnish

FOR THE APPLESAUCE

3 Pippin, McIntosh, or other firm
    crisp apples, peeled, cored and sliced
2 tablespoons water
granulated sugar, to taste

1 Grate the potatoes and onion on a medium-coarse grater, or using the grating attachment on a food processor if you have one. Mix with the rosemary and add salt and black pepper to taste.

2 Heat 2 tablespoons of the olive oil in an 11 inch skillet. Add the potato mixture and press down firmly. Sauté for 8 minutes, or until the underside is crisp and golden. Slide the rosti out onto a plate, then invert another plate on top and turn them over. Heat the remaining oil in the pan, then slide the rosti back into the pan with the cooked side uppermost, and cook for another 8 minutes.

3 While the rosti is cooking, make the applesauce. Put the apples into a saucepan with the water, bring to a boil, then reduce the heat, cover, and cook gently for 5–10 minutes, until the apples have collapsed. Mash lightly with a wooden spoon and sweeten to taste with granulated sugar.

4 Turn the rosti out of the skillet onto a large serving plate and garnish with a few rosemary sprigs. Serve in thick slices, with the applesauce.

South American pinto & pumpkin casserole ⓥ

SERVES 4
PREPARATION 15 MINUTES
COOKING 15 MINUTES

4 cups skinned, seeded, and cubed
   pumpkin or butternut squash
   (½ inch cubes)
4 garlic cloves
4 cups vegetable stock
1 tablespoon olive oil
2 large onions, finely chopped
2 large red bell peppers, cored,
   seeded, and diced
2 teaspoons dried epazote or basil
kernels cut from 1 corn cob,
   or 1 cup frozen corn kernels
2 (15 oz) cans pinto beans
2–3 tablespoons lemon juice
salt and black pepper
1 tablespoon finely chopped fresh
   epazote or flat leaf parsley, to garnish
warm bread, to serve

1 Put the cubes of pumpkin or squash into a large saucepan with the garlic and stock. Bring to a boil, then reduce the heat, cover, and simmer for about 15 minutes, or until the pumpkin is tender. Transfer the contents of the pan to a food processor and blend to a thin puree.

2 While the pumpkin is cooking, heat the olive oil in another large saucepan. Add the onions, bell peppers, and dried epazote or basil, cover, and cook over gentle heat for 15 minutes, or until the vegetables are tender and slightly caramelized.

3 Add the pumpkin puree to the vegetables in the pan, along with the corn kernels and the pinto beans and their liquid. Stir over gentle heat until hot, then add the lemon juice and salt and black pepper to taste.

4 Ladle into warmed bowls, sprinkle with fresh epazote or parsley, and serve with warm country-style bread (I love a dark whole-wheat or walnut bread with this—not very South American, but very good).

Squash stuffed with Moroccan rice

Mini squash can be used, but they need to be large enough to be baked in halves and then stuffed, because that way they cook really well.

SERVES 4
PREPARATION 20 MINUTES
COOKING 30 MINUTES

2 small squash
1 garlic clove, crushed
olive oil, for greasing
salt

FOR THE RICE FILLING

1 cup white basmati rice or other
  long-grain rice
3 tablespoons raisins
1 tablespoon butter
1½ teaspoons ras el hanout
  (see page 295)
½ teaspoon turmeric
2 tablespoons lemon juice
8 green queen olives, pitted and
  chopped
½ cup chopped cilantro

1 Cut the squash in half through their stems. Scoop out the seeds, then rub the cut surfaces of the squash with garlic and salt. Place cut side down on a well-oiled baking sheet and bake in a preheated oven, at 400°F, for 30 minutes, or until the squash can easily be pierced with the point of a knife.

2 Meanwhile, make the rice filling. Bring half a saucepan of water to a boil, add the rice, and bring back to a boil, then reduce the heat and simmer, uncovered, for 8–10 minutes, or according to the package directions, until the rice is tender but still has some resistance.

3 Plump the raisins by soaking them in boiling water for 2–3 minutes.

4 Drain the rice. Return to the pan with the butter, ras el hanout, turmeric, and lemon juice and mix well. Drain the raisins and add to the rice, along with the chopped olives and cilantro. Taste and season with salt.

5 Turn the squash so that they are cavity side uppermost, then fill the cavities with the rice mixture, piling it up. Serve immediately, or cover with aluminum foil and keep warm in the oven for a few minutes before serving.

Whole baked Brie in phyllo with apricot sauce

SERVES 6
PREPARATION 15 MINUTES,
 PLUS STANDING
COOKING 30–40 MINUTES

1 (1 lb) package phyllo pastry
¼–⅓ cup olive oil
1 whole Brie cheese, 8–10 inches
 in diameter, firm and underripe,
 if possible
mashed potatoes and green beans,
 to serve

FOR THE SAUCE

1½ cups apricot preserves
¼ cup lemon juice

1 Place a sheet of phyllo pastry large enough to hold the Brie on a baking sheet and brush the pastry with olive oil. Place another sheet overlapping it, and brush with more oil. The idea is to make a square of phyllo that is big enough to form a base for the Brie and that can also be brought up the sides. It's better to have too large a square than too small, because you will be trimming off excess pastry later.

2 Put the Brie on top of the phyllo, then cut the phyllo, allowing about 4 inches all round the Brie. Now, build up more layers of phyllo on top of the Brie—this layer needs to cover the cheese with about 2 inches to spare around the sides. Fold up the bottom layer of phyllo to meet the top layer and roll them together to secure them and form a decorative seal all around the Brie. Brush with more oil and make a steam hole in the middle.

3 You can scrunch up some of the phyllo scraps or cut ribbons out of them, brush with oil, and use to decorate the top of the pie in any way that you desire. The pie will keep in a cool place for several hours.

4 When you're ready to bake the Brie, place it, on its baking sheet, in a preheated oven, at 400°F, and bake for 30–40 minutes, until the pastry is golden brown and crisp. Remove from the oven and let it stand for 10–15 minutes to settle, then slide carefully onto a large plate. It looks fantastic, but once cut, the Brie will ooze all over the place, so make sure it's on a large enough plate, preferably with sides, or on a plate standing on a tray.

5 To make the apricot sauce, put the apricot preserves and lemon juice into a small saucepan and bring to a boil. Pour into a pitcher to serve. Serve the mashed potatoes and green beans separately.

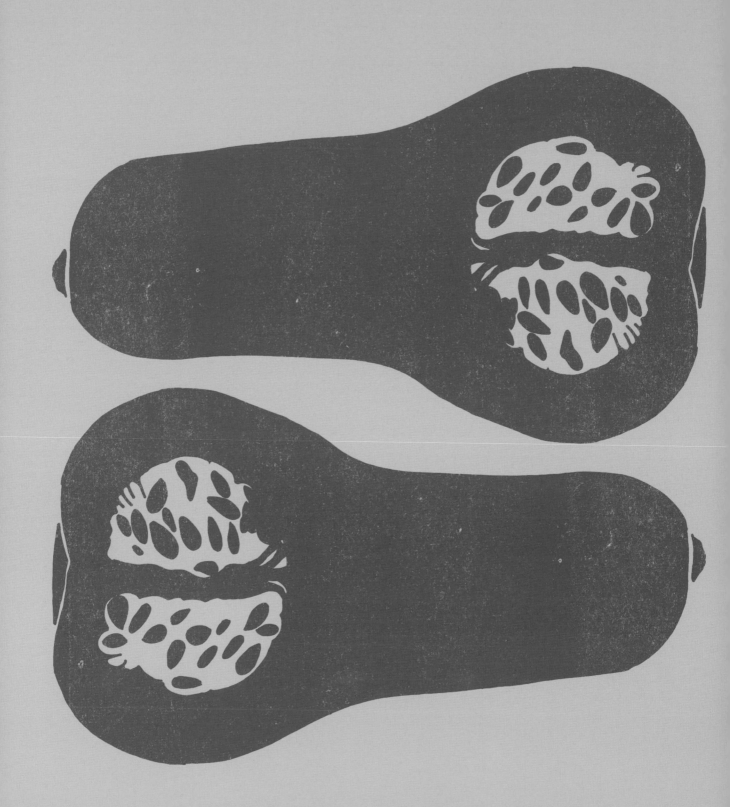

Dinners to impress

Red pepper, ricotta & fennel tortellini with tarragon sauce

SERVES 4

PREPARATION 45 MINUTES,
  PLUS RESTING

COOKING 30 MINUTES

FOR THE PASTA DOUGH

2¾ cups all-purpose white flour
pinch of salt
3 eggs
1 tablespoon olive oil

FOR THE FILLING

1 fennel bulb, trimmed
1 large red bell pepper, halved, cored,
  and seeded
1 garlic clove, crushed
½ cup ricotta cheese
1 cup grated Parmesan-style cheese
salt and black pepper

FOR THE TARRAGON SAUCE

½ cup vegetable stock
  (use the fennel water)
½ cup dry white wine
2 cups heavy cream
2 good leafy tarragon sprigs,
  chopped

1 To make the pasta dough, put the flour, salt, eggs, and olive oil into a food processor and blend until combined. Gradually add enough cold water—maybe ¼–⅓ cup—to make a soft, malleable dough. Remove from the food processor and knead on a lightly floured board for a few minutes, until smooth, glossy, and pliable, then put into a plastic bag and let rest for 1 hour.

2 Meanwhile, make the filling. Run a potato peeler down the outside of the fennel to remove any potentially stringy parts. Quarter the fennel and cook in a saucepan of boiling water for 8–10 minutes, until tender. Strain; the water makes wonderful stock so save it for the sauce.

3 Grill the red bell pepper, cut side down, under a hot broiler for about 10 minutes, or until black and blistered in places. Cool, then strip off the skin.

4 Chop the cooked fennel and red bell pepper finely. Add the garlic, ricotta, and Parmesan and season with salt and black pepper. Divide the mixture into 20 equal portions.

5 To make the tortellini, divide the pasta dough into 20 equal portions. Take one portion and roll out on a floured board, making it as thin as you can—big enough to cut out 2 circles with a 2½ inch cutter. Continue with the rest of the dough, then take 2 of the circles and put a portion of filling in the center of one. Brush the edges with cold water and place the second circle on top, pressing down the edges well. Set aside and repeat the process with the rest of the circles and filling.

6 Bring a large saucepan of water to a boil. Drop in the tortellini and cook for about 6 minutes, or until the pasta is tender.

7 Meanwhile, to make the tarragon sauce, put the stock, wine, and cream into a saucepan and boil until reduced by half and slightly thickened. Remove from the heat, season, and add the tarragon.

8 Drain the pasta gently in a colander, then transfer to a warmed dish, pour over the tarragon sauce, and serve.

Chestnut-stuffed onions with porcini gravy

Using cornmeal here instead of traditional bread crumbs keeps the stuffing moist while preventing it from getting soggy.

SERVES 6
PREPARATION 30 MINUTES
COOKING 40–50 MINUTES

6 large onions
1 tablespoon olive oil, plus extra
   for brushing
1 tablespoon butter
1 celery heart, chopped
4–6 garlic cloves, finely chopped
3 (8 oz) vacuum-packs or cans whole
   chestnuts, drained if necessary
1 tablespoon chopped thyme
2 tablespoons cornmeal
salt and black pepper
thyme sprigs, to garnish

FOR THE GRAVY

½ oz dried porcini
3 cups vegetable stock
2 tablespoons olive oil
1 onion, chopped
4 garlic cloves, finely chopped
2 tablespoons whole-wheat flour
2 tablespoons soy sauce
2 tablespoons medium red wine

1 Cut the onions in half horizontally and trim them slightly, if necessary, to make them stand level. Using a sharp knife, cut out most of the centers, leaving about 3 good layers on the outside. Brush these onion "cups" all over with olive oil and place in a shallow casserole dish.

2 Chop the scooped-out onion. Heat the olive oil and butter in a large saucepan, add the chopped onion, celery, and garlic, cover, and cook gently without browning for 10–15 minutes, or until tender. Remove from the heat.

3 Add the chestnuts to the onion mixture in the pan, mashing them a little, then stir in the thyme and cornmeal and add salt and black pepper to taste. Divide the mixture among the onion "cups," piling it up well, and bake in a preheated oven, at 400°F, for 30–35 minutes, until the onion "cups" are tender—cover the casserole dish with aluminum foil if the stuffing seems to be drying out before this.

4 While the onions are cooking, make the gravy. Put the mushrooms into a saucepan with the stock. Bring to a boil, then cover and let soak for 15–20 minutes. Strain, reserving the liquid. Chop the mushrooms finely.

5 Heat the olive oil in a saucepan, add the onion, and cook for 10 minutes, until tender and lightly browned. Add the chopped mushrooms and garlic and sauté for another 1–2 minutes, then stir in the flour and cook to brown it a little. Pour in the reserved porcini liquid, the soy sauce, and red wine and stir over the heat until thickened.

6 For a really smooth sauce, you can now puree the whole lot in a food processor or blender (or strain it through a strainer) or, if you prefer some texture, leave it as it is.

7 Let the gravy simmer gently for 10 minutes, then add salt and black pepper to taste. Serve the stuffed onions with the porcini gravy and sprigs of thyme.

Brie & cranberry souffles

You won't need the full quantity of cranberry sauce for this, but it's not worth making less—serve the remainder with the souffles, or keep it in a jar in the refrigerator for up to 4 weeks.

SERVES 4
PREPARATION 30 MINUTES
COOKING 40 MINUTES

FOR THE CRANBERRY SAUCE

2 cups cranberries
⅔ cup granulated sugar

FOR THE SOUFFLES

1 tablespoon butter, plus extra for
   greasing
1 tablespoon all-purpose white flour
½ cup milk
1 teaspoon Dijon mustard
⅓ cup shredded cheddar cheese
pinch of white pepper
3 egg whites
2 egg yolks
3½ oz Brie cheese, not too ripe,
   thinly sliced
salt

1 First, make the cranberry sauce. Wash the cranberries, then place them in a saucepan with just the water clinging to them and heat gently for 10 minutes, or until soft. Add the sugar and simmer gently for about 15 minutes, or until "jammy." Set aside.

2 Melt the butter in a saucepan and stir in the flour. Cook for 1 minute, stirring, then remove from the heat and gradually stir in the milk. Bring to a boil and cook, stirring, until the sauce thickens, then remove from the heat and stir in the mustard, cheddar, white pepper, and a little salt. Let cool slightly.

3 Whisk the egg whites in a large, clean, grease-free bowl, until they stand in soft peaks. Stir the egg yolks into the cheese mixture, then stir in 1 tablespoon of the whisked whites to loosen the mixture. Gently fold in the rest of the egg whites.

4 Generously grease four ⅔ cup ramekins or individual souffle dishes. Put 1 tablespoon of the mixture into each dish, then cover with 1–2 slices of Brie and 1–2 teaspoons of the cranberry sauce. Spoon the rest of the souffle mixture on top—it can come to the top of the dishes but no higher.

5 Stand the dishes in a roasting pan, then pour in boiling water to come halfway up the sides of the dishes. Bake in a preheated oven, at 350°F, for 13–15 minutes, until risen and golden brown and a toothpick inserted into the center of a souffle comes out clean. Serve at once.

Croustade of asparagus hollandaise

To save yourself a last minute rush when you're expecting guests, you can make the base in advance and refrigerate or even freeze it, either before or after baking.

SERVES 6
PREPARATION 30 MINUTES
COOKING 20–25 MINUTES

2 lb asparagus tips (thin if possible), trimmed

FOR THE CROUSTADE

3 cups soft white bread crumbs
1¼ cups cashew nuts, finely ground in a coffee grinder (or use ground almonds or almond meal)
1¼ sticks butter
3 garlic cloves, finely chopped
1 small onion, finely grated
1 cup pine nuts
5 teaspoons water

FOR THE HOLLANDAISE SAUCE

2 sticks butter, cut into chunks
4 egg yolks
2 tablespoons lemon juice
salt and black pepper

1 First, make the croustade. Mix together the bread crumbs, ground nuts, butter, garlic, and onion by hand or by processing in a food processor, then stir in the pine nuts and water and mix to make a dough.

2 Press the mixture down lightly into the bottom of a 12 inch shallow, ovenproof or pizza dish. Bake in a preheated oven, at 400°F, for 15–20 minutes, until crisp and golden brown. Set aside.

3 Cook the asparagus in a little boiling water in a saucepan for 3–4 minutes, or until tender, then drain.

4 Meanwhile, make the sauce. Melt the butter gently in a saucepan without browning it. Put the egg yolks, lemon juice, and some seasoning into a food processor or blender and process for 1 minute until thick. With the motor running, pour in the melted butter in a thin, steady stream—the sauce will thicken. Let stand for a minute or two.

5 Pile the asparagus on top of the croustade, pour the sauce over it, and serve immediately.

Eggplant schnitzels with watercress sauce ⓥ

Thick slices of broiled eggplant sandwiched with smoked tofu and arame—a delicately flavored seaweed—give these schnitzels a gorgeous juiciness and smoky flavor, encased in a crisp crumb coating.

SERVES 4
PREPARATION 30 MINUTES,
   PLUS SOAKING
COOKING 25 MINUTES

¼ oz arame seaweed
2 eggplants, stems trimmed
olive oil, for brushing and
   pan-frying
1 (8 oz) block smoked tofu, drained
⅓ cup plus 2 teaspoons cornstarch
⅓ cup water
¼ cup dried bread crumbs
salt and black pepper
lemon slices, to serve

FOR THE WATERCRESS SAUCE

bunch or package of watercress
1 cup light cream or
   unsweetened soy cream
1 teaspoon cornstarch

1 Put the arame into a bowl, cover with cold water, and let soak for 10 minutes.

2 Meanwhile, cut the eggplants lengthwise into 4 slices—or in half, then in half again. (Two of the slices will have skin on one side.) Brush the cut surfaces of the eggplant with olive oil, place on a broiler pan, and cook under a preheated hot broiler until they are lightly browned and feel tender to the point of a knife, turning them over when the first side is done.

3 Drain the arame, then puree it with the tofu in a food processor or using an immersion blender. Season with salt and black pepper, then spread some of the mixture thickly on a slice of eggplant and press another slice on top to make a fat sandwich. Repeat with all the slices, dividing the tofu mixture evenly among them.

4 Put the cornstarch into a bowl and mix in the water to make a thick coating paste. Dip each eggplant sandwich into the paste, then into the bread crumbs, making sure it's thoroughly coated. Heat a little olive oil in a skillet and cook the schnitzels on both sides. Drain on paper towels.

5 To make the watercress sauce, puree the watercress, cream, and cornstarch in a food processor or using an immersion blender. Heat gently, stirring, until the sauce has thickened.

6 Serve the schnitzels with slices of lemon and accompanied by the watercress sauce.

Carrot, parsnip & chestnut terrine with red wine gravy

SERVES 4

PREPARATION 30 MINUTES

COOKING 1 HOUR 5 MINUTES

3 garlic cloves, chopped

4 tablespoons butter, softened

2 tablespoons dried bread crumbs

2 tablespoons olive oil

2 onions, chopped

2 parsnips, cut into 1½ inch chunks

3 carrots, sliced into circles

1 bulb of fennel, trimmed
    and chopped

1 teaspoon caraway seeds

10 vacuum-packed or canned whole
    peeled chestnuts, drained if
    necessary, coarsely chopped

1½ cups fine soft whole-wheat
    bread crumbs

¼ cup lemon juice

2 tablespoons shoyu or tamari

3 eggs, beaten

2 tablespoons chopped parsley

salt and black pepper

FOR THE RED WINE GRAVY

1 tablespoon olive oil

2 onions, finely chopped

2 tablespoons all-purpose white flour

1 cup vegetable stock

1 cup red wine

2 tablespoons shoyu or tamari

sugar, to taste

1 Line a 9 x 5 x 3 inch loaf pan with a strip of nonstick parchment paper. Mix the garlic with the butter and use half of this to grease the lined bottom and sides of the pan, then coat the bottom and sides with half the dried bread crumbs.

2 Heat the olive oil in a large saucepan, add the onions, parsnips, carrots, and fennel, cover, and cook gently for about 20 minutes, stirring from time to time, or until all the vegetables are tender.

3 Add the caraway seeds and cook for a minute or two longer, then remove from the heat and mix in the chestnuts, soft bread crumbs, lemon juice, shoyu or tamari, eggs, parsley, and some salt and black pepper.

4 Spoon the mixture into the prepared loaf pan and level the surface. Sprinkle the top with the rest of the dried bread crumbs and dot with the remaining garlic butter. Bake in a preheated oven, at 350°F, for 40 minutes, until firm on top and a toothpick inserted into the center comes out clean.

5 While the loaf is cooking, make the gravy. Heat the olive oil in a skillet, add the onions, and cook for 10 minutes, until they are tender and lightly browned. Add the flour and stir over the heat for 3–4 minutes, until nut brown—the mixture will be dry. Stir in the stock and wine, then simmer over moderate heat until thickened. Add the shoyu or tamari and season with salt, black pepper, and perhaps a touch of sugar. Serve as it is or, if you prefer smooth gravy, strain it through a strainer. Either way, add more stock if you want it thinner.

6 Serve the terrine in thick slices with the red wine gravy.

Dauphinoise roulade with red chard & blue cheese filling

This wonderful, unusual roulade can be made in advance, ready for reheating just before serving, when it will become crisp and gorgeous. A tomato sauce, such as the one on page 20, and fine green beans go well with it.

SERVES 4
PREPARATION 40 MINUTES
COOKING 55 MINUTES

FOR THE ROULADE

olive oil, for greasing and brushing
7 red-skinned or white round potatoes,
   peeled and thinly sliced
1 garlic clove, crushed
salt and black pepper
green salad, to serve

FOR THE FILLING

1 lb red chard, leaves
   and stems separated
6 oz blue cheese, coarsely chopped

1 Line an 8½ x 12½ inch jellyroll pan with nonstick parchment paper and brush with olive oil. Mix the potatoes with the garlic and some salt and black pepper, arrange them carefully and evenly in the pan, and brush with olive oil. Cover with a piece of nonstick parchment paper and bake in a preheated oven, at 400°F, for 30 minutes, then remove the paper and bake for another 5–10 minutes, until the potatoes are tender and golden brown. Cool and set aside.

2 Meanwhile, chop the chard stems, then cook in a saucepan of boiling water for 5 minutes to soften. Add the leaves, cover, and cook for 7–10 minutes, until tender. Drain well, then mix with the blue cheese.

3 Turn out the roulade onto its covering piece of parchment paper. Cover the surface with the chard mixture. Starting with one of the short edges, carefully roll up the roulade, using the paper underneath to help—it rolls up easily and you don't need to be gentle with it.

4 Put the roulade on a heatproof serving dish. About 15 minutes before you want to serve it, put the roulade back into the oven, uncovered, until heated through and crisp and golden on the outside. Serve immediately, with a green salad.

Pea & mint timbales with baby vegetables & Parmesan chips

SERVES 6

PREPARATION 40 MINUTES

COOKING 1¼ HOURS

1 tablespoon butter, melted

1–2 tablespoons finely grated
  Parmesan-style cheese

3 cups frozen peas

¼ cup chopped mint

⅔ cup heavy cream

1 cup light cream

2 egg yolks

4 eggs

grated nutmeg

salt and black pepper

FOR THE PARMESAN CHIPS

3 tablespoons finely grated
  Parmesan-style cheese

FOR THE BRAISED VEGETABLES

1 tablespoon olive oil

2 tablespoons butter

1 lb baby carrots

1 lb tiny new potatoes

8 oz trimmed baby fennel

⅓ cup water

1 cup asparagus tips

2 cups sugarsnap peas

1 cup shelled fava beans

1 Brush six ⅔ cup individual ramekins generously with melted butter, then dust liberally with Parmesan.

2 To make the timbales, cook the peas and half the mint in a saucepan of boiling water for 2–3 minutes, or until tender. Drain, then puree in a food processor with the two creams. Add the egg yolks and whole eggs and blend again. Pour the mixture into a strainer set over a bowl and push through as much as you can—discard the residue. Season with nutmeg, salt, and black pepper, then pour into the prepared ramekins.

3 Stand the ramekins in a deep roasting pan, then pour in boiling water to come halfway up the sides of the dishes. Bake in a preheated oven, at 350°F, for 40–45 minutes, or until a toothpick inserted into the center comes out clean. Remove and set aside.

4 To make the chips, line a baking sheet with nonstick parchment paper. Put ½ tablespoon of the Parmesan on the paper and spread it into a 3 inch circle. Repeat to make 5 more circles of cheese. Increase the oven temperature to 400°F, and bake for about 5 minutes, or until the Parmesan is golden brown and crisp. Let cool.

5 Next, cook the vegetables. Heat the olive oil and butter in a large saucepan and add the carrots, potatoes, fennel, and water. Bring to a boil, then reduce the heat, cover, and simmer for 15 minutes. Add the asparagus, sugarsnaps, and fava beans, then simmer for another 10 minutes, until all the vegetables are tender. Season with salt and black pepper.

6 Arrange the vegetables on warmed individual plates and sprinkle with the remaining chopped mint. Turn out the timbales—they will come out easily—arrange on plates and top each with a Parmesan chip.

Tomato, pesto & mozzarella tart with walnut pastry

The reason for using tomatoes on the vine in this recipe is for flavor instead of appearance, although they do look especially attractive in this tart.

SERVES 6
PREPARATION 30 MINUTES,
    PLUS CHILLING
COOKING 1¾ HOURS

3 cups whole-wheat flour or
    half whole-wheat, half white
1½ sticks butter, cut into
    coarse chunks
½ teaspoon salt
½ cup finely chopped walnuts
3 tablespoons cold water
2 tablespoons olive oil

FOR THE FILLING

2¼ lb baby tomatoes on the vine
1 tablespoon balsamic vinegar
1 red onion, sliced
1 tablespoon olive oil
4 garlic cloves, sliced
4 teaspoons pesto
5 oz mozzarella cheese, drained
    and cut into ½ inch pieces
12 ripe black olives, preferably
    Kalamata, pitted
salt and black pepper

1 Take the tomatoes off the vine and put them into a roasting pan. Pour the balsamic vinegar over them and bake in a preheated oven, at 400°F, for 45–50 minutes, or until they are bursting and blackened in places.

2 Meanwhile, make the pastry. Put the flour, butter, and salt into a food processor and blend until the mixture resembles coarse bread crumbs. Alternatively, put the ingredients into a bowl and rub the butter into the flour with your fingertips. Add the walnuts and water and mix to a dough.

3 Turn out the dough onto a lightly floured surface. Knead briefly, then shape into a circle and roll out to fit an 11–12 inch shallow, round tart pan. Trim the edges, prick the bottom thoroughly all over, then chill for 30 minutes.

4 Continue with the filling. Sauté the onion in the olive oil for 10–15 minutes, until soft and sweet. Add the garlic and remove from the heat.

5 Bake the tart in the oven at the same temperature as for the tomatoes for 20 minutes, until the pastry is "set" and lightly browned. A minute or two before you take it out of the oven, heat the remaining 2 tablespoons of olive oil in a small saucepan until smoking hot. As soon as the tart comes out of the oven, pour the hot olive oil all over the bottom—it will sizzle and almost "fry." This will "waterproof" the bottom of the tart so that it will remain crisp.

6 Just before you want to serve the tart, put the onion mixture and the roasted tomatoes into the tart shell. Season with salt and black pepper, remembering that both the pesto and the mozzarella are salty. Drizzle with pesto, then arrange the mozzarella and olives on top. Bake in a preheated oven, at 350°F, for 25 minutes, or until the mozzarella has melted and browned in places.

Celeriac rosti with green beans in almond butter ⓥ

SERVES 4
PREPARATION 30 MINUTES
COOKING 20 MINUTES

1 large celeriac, peeled and grated
1 cup slivered almonds
2–4 tablespoons olive oil
salt and black pepper

FOR THE BEANS

2¼ cups thin green beans,
  lightly trimmed and cut in half
4 teaspoons roasted almond butter
  (see page 294)

1 Mix the celeriac with the almonds and some salt and black pepper.

2 Heat 2 tablespoons of the olive oil in a skillet large enough to hold four 8 inch metal baking rings—or you may need to use 2 skillets. Place the rings in the skillet or pans and fill with the celeriac mixture, dividing it evenly between them and pressing down well. Cover with a plate or lid and cook over gentle heat for about 10 minutes, or until the underside is golden brown.

3 Using a spatula, flip each rosti over (still in its ring) and press down the mixture so that it is touching the surface of the skillet. Cover as before and cook the other side.

4 Meanwhile, bring a 1 inch depth of water to a boil in a saucepan. Add the green beans, bring back to a boil, and cook for 3–4 minutes, or until just tender. Drain, return to the pan, and toss with the almond butter and some salt and black pepper.

5 Place a celeriac rosti on each plate and top with green beans. Slip off the rings and serve.

Toor dhal with lime & cilantro leaf dumplings

The dumplings are very British, but with the fresh Asian flavorings they seem made to go with this dish perfectly.

SERVES 4
PREPARATION 20 MINUTES
COOKING 1¼ HOURS

FOR THE DHAL

2 cups toor dhal (see page 296), thoroughly washed in hot water and drained
8½ cups water
2 tablespoons olive oil
2 whole cloves
1 cinnamon stick
1–2 dried red chiles
6 dried kaffir lime leaves
1 whole green chile
1 (14½ oz) can diced tomatoes
1 tablespoon garam masala
1 tablespoon lemon juice
½–1 tablespoon sugar
salt and black pepper

FOR THE CILANTRO DUMPLINGS

1 cup all-purpose flour
1 teaspoon baking powder
2 teaspoons cumin seeds
½ cup chopped cilantro
finely grated zest of 1 lime
¼ cup olive oil
¼ cup water

1   Put the toor dhal into a large saucepan with the water and bring to a boil. Using a slotted spoon, scoop off the foam, then reduce the heat, cover, and let cook gently for about 1 hour, until soft.

2   Meanwhile, heat the olive oil in a medium saucepan and add the cloves, cinnamon stick, and dried chiles. Let them sizzle for about half a minute, then add the lime leaves and sizzle again. Stir in the green chile, cook for a few more seconds, then add the tomatoes. Bring to a boil, then reduce the heat and let simmer, uncovered, for 15–20 minutes, or until thick, stirring often to prevent it from sticking. Remove the cinnamon stick, chile, and any large pieces of lime leaf.

3   Stir the dhal to give a creamy consistency, then add the tomato mixture, garam masala, lemon juice, sugar to taste, and some salt and black pepper.

4   To make the dumplings, put the flour and baking powder into a bowl, add all the remaining ingredients with salt to taste, and mix quickly to a soft dough. Form into 8 dumplings. Bring the dhal to a gentle boil and drop in the dumplings. Reduce the heat, cover, and cook for about 15 minutes, or until the dumplings have risen to the surface and are cooked inside. Serve from the pot or carefully transfer to a warmed casserole.

Lentil cakes in citrus broth ⓥ

SERVES 4
PREPARATION 1 HOUR
COOKING 55–60 MINUTES

FOR THE LENTIL CAKES

1½ cups green lentils
1 onion, coarsely chopped
3¾ cups water
½ cup chopped fresh cilantro
1 tablespoon ground coriander
juice of 1½ limes
olive oil, for pan-frying
salt and black pepper

FOR THE BROTH

2½ cups vegetable stock
2 lemon grass stalks, crushed
green tops from a bunch of
    scallions
3–4 kaffir lime leaves
2 garlic cloves
½ cup chopped fresh cilantro

1 Put the lentils into a saucepan with the onion and water. Bring to a boil, then reduce the heat, cover, and simmer gently for 40–45 minutes, or according to the package directions, until the lentils are tender and all the water has been absorbed. Add a little more water toward the end of cooking if the lentils are sticking, but make sure no water remains.

2 Mash the lentils with the fresh and ground coriander, the lime juice, and some salt and black pepper. Form into 12 cakes, pressing the mixture so it holds together. Heat a little olive oil in a skillet and cook the lentil cakes on both sides until crisp and browned.

3 To make the broth, put the stock into a saucepan with the lemon grass, scallion tops, lime leaves, and garlic. Bring to a boil, then reduce the heat and simmer, uncovered, for a few minutes, until the liquid has reduced by half. Strain, discard the flavorings, and return the stock to the pan with the chopped cilantro.

4 Serve the lentil cakes in shallow bowls in a pool of the broth.

Tea-smoked chestnut risotto

SERVES 4

PREPARATION 20 MINUTES,
   PLUS SMOKING

COOKING 35–40 MINUTES

FOR THE TEA-SMOKED CHESTNUTS

½ cup uncooked rice
¼ cup firmly packed dark brown sugar
⅓ cup black tea leaves
1 tablespoon whole allspice
2 tablespoons molasses
1 cinnamon stick
20 vacuum-packed or canned
   whole peeled chestnuts, drained
   if necessary

FOR THE RISOTTO

4 cups vegetable stock
1 tablespoon olive oil
2 onions, finely chopped
2 celery sticks, finely chopped
2 garlic cloves, finely chopped
2 cups risotto rice
1¼ cups dry white wine
4 tablespoons butter
1 cup grated Parmesan-style cheese
salt and black pepper

1 Smoke the chestnuts an hour or so in advance. Line a wok with aluminum foil, then put in all the ingredients except for the chestnuts and stir gently.

2 Arrange a rack over the wok and place the chestnuts on top. Cover with foil and cook over medium heat for 10 minutes, then remove from the heat and let stand, covered, for another 10 minutes.

3 Meanwhile, make the risotto. Put the stock into a saucepan and bring to a boil, then reduce the heat and keep hot over gentle heat.

4 Heat the olive oil in a large saucepan, add the onions and celery, and stir, then cover and cook gently for 7–8 minutes, until tender but not browned. Stir in the garlic and cook for a minute or two longer.

5 Add the rice to the pan and stir over gentle heat for 2–3 minutes, then pour in the wine and stir all the time as it simmers away.

6 When the wine has disappeared, add a ladleful of the hot stock. Stir over low-to-medium heat until the rice has absorbed the stock, then add another ladleful, and continue in this way for 15–20 minutes, until you've used all the stock and the rice is tender and a creamy consistency.

7 Stir in the butter, smoked chestnuts, and half the Parmesan, season with salt and black pepper, and serve, sprinkled with the rest of the cheese.

Butternut squash with porcini & garlic stuffing & mashed celeriac ⓥ

SERVES 6
PREPARATION 20 MINUTES
COOKING 45 MINUTES

2 oz dried porcini
6 fat garlic cloves
¼ cup olive oil
2 butternut squashes
salt and black pepper
flat leaf parsley sprigs, to garnish

FOR THE MASHED CELERIAC

1 large head of celeriac, cut into
  even pieces
4 russet or Yukon gold potatoes,
  peeled and cut into even pieces
2 tablespoons olive oil

1 Put the porcini into a saucepan, cover with water, and bring to a boil. Boil for about 2 minutes, or until just tender. Drain—the liquid isn't needed for this recipe, but you could freeze it for later because it makes fantastic stock for soups and gravies.

2 Put the porcini into a food processor with the garlic, 3 tablespoons of the olive oil, and a seasoning of salt and black pepper and process to a coarse puree.

3 Cut the butternut squashes in half lengthwise, down through the stem. Scoop out the seeds with a teaspoon and discard. Rub the remaining olive oil and a little salt into the flesh, then fill the cavities with the porcini mixture, dividing it among all 4 of the halves.

4 Put the butternut squash halves, cut side down, onto a baking sheet and bake in a preheated oven, at 400°F, for about 40 minutes, or until you can insert a sharp pointed knife easily into the skin and the flesh inside feels tender.

5 While the squashes are cooking, make the mashed celeriac. Put the celeriac and potatoes into a saucepan, cover with water, and bring to a boil, then reduce the heat and simmer for 15–20 minutes, or until tender. Drain, reserving the liquid (this, too, makes fabulous stock). Mash or puree in a food processor with the olive oil, salt, and black pepper and enough of the reserved liquid to make a soft, creamy consistency.

6 To serve, carefully lift the squashes off the baking sheet, making sure that the stuffing isn't left behind. Cut each squash half in two and place on a serving dish—they look good arranged like the rays of the sun on a large, flat, round plate—and garnish with a few parsley sprigs. Serve the mashed celeriac separately.

Tagliatelle with leek & morel cream & crisp garlic

SERVES 4
PREPARATION 20 MINUTES
COOKING 30 MINUTES

1 lb tagliatelle
2 tablespoons olive oil
4 large garlic cloves, cut into
   thin slices, to serve

FOR THE CREAM SAUCE

2 tablespoons butter
1 tablespoon olive oil
7 oz morel mushrooms or
   ¾ oz dried morels (see page 296),
   rehydrated according to package
   directions, coarsely chopped
2 garlic cloves, crushed
2½ cups light cream, heavy cream,
   or half-and-half
3 cups finely sliced leeks
2 tablespoons chopped parsley
salt and black pepper

1 To make the sauce, heat the butter and olive oil in a saucepan. Add the morels and crushed garlic and cook gently for 5–10 minutes, until any liquid they produce has boiled away. Pour in the cream and simmer, uncovered, until reduced by half.

2 Cook the leeks in a saucepan of boiling water for 3–4 minutes, then drain (the water makes tasty stock) in a colander and rinse under cold water to preserve the color. Drain well, then add to the cream mixture along with the parsley and some salt and black pepper.

3 Bring a large saucepan of water to a boil for the pasta. When it comes to a boil, add the tagliatelle and cook according to the package directions. Drain into a colander and return to the hot saucepan with 1 tablespoon of the olive oil.

4 While the pasta is cooking, heat the remaining olive oil in a small skillet, add the sliced garlic, and sauté for a few seconds until golden and crisp—be careful not to let it burn and become bitter. Set aside.

5 Add the leek and morel sauce to the pasta in the pan and serve on warmed dishes, or serve the pasta first, then spoon the sauce on top. Either way, sprinkle with the crisp garlic and serve immediately.

Chickpea flatcake topped with lemon- & honey-roasted vegetables

![decorative rule]

SERVES 4–6
PREPARATION 30 MINUTES
COOKING 45 MINUTES

¼ cup olive oil, plus extra for greasing
3 large onions, finely chopped
3 large garlic cloves, crushed
2 teaspoons cumin seeds
3 (15 oz) cans chickpeas,
    drained and rinsed
salt and black pepper
flat leaf parsley sprig, chopped,
    to garnish

FOR THE ROASTED VEGETABLES

1¾ lb Jerusalem artichokes, peeled
    and cut into 1 inch chunks
7 carrots, cleaned and cut into sticks
3 tablespoons olive oil
3 tablespoons honey
3 tablespoons lemon juice
grated zest of 1 lemon

1 Start with the roasted vegetables. Put the artichokes and carrots into a roasting pan with the olive oil, honey, lemon juice and zest, and some salt and black pepper and mix gently. Roast in a preheated oven, at 350°F, for about 45 minutes, turning the vegetables from time to time.

2 Meanwhile, make the flatcake. Heat 2 tablespoons of the olive oil in a saucepan, add the onions, cover, and sauté gently for 10 minutes. Add the garlic and cumin seeds and cook for another 2–3 minutes. Remove from the heat and add the chickpeas and some salt and black pepper. Mash the mixture thoroughly.

3 Put the mixture into a lightly oiled 12 inch loose-bottom, round tart pan and smooth the surface. Cover with aluminum foil and bake for about 15 minutes, then remove the foil, pour the remaining olive oil over the top, and bake for another 5–10 minutes, until golden—but don't let it get dry. Remove from the oven. Turn the flatcake out of the pan and slide it onto a warm serving dish. Spoon the roasted vegetables on top, garnish with parsley, and serve.

Stilton, apple & sage crepes with berry sauce

SERVES 4

PREPARATION 30 MINUTES

COOKING 30 MINUTES

1 tablespoon olive oil

1½ cups chopped shallots

2 Pippin or other crisp sweet apples,
   peeled and chopped

1 cup fine soft white bread crumbs

5 oz Stilton cheese or other blue
   cheese, crumbled

1 tablespoon chopped sage

8 crepes, made according to the
   fajita recipe on page 189,
   omitting the sugar,

2 eggs, beaten

cornmeal, for coating

canola oil or peanut oil, for
   deep-frying

salt and black pepper

red Swiss chard leaves, to garnish

FOR THE BLACKBERRY SAUCE

¼ cup blackberry jelly or preserves

1 teaspoon Dijon mustard

2 tablespoons each orange juice
   and lemon juice

¼ cup port

1 Heat the olive oil in a skillet, add the shallots, and cook for 5 minutes, then add the apples, cover, and cook for another 5–10 minutes, or until the shallots and apples are tender. Remove from the heat and add the bread crumbs, Stilton, and sage, then season with salt and black pepper.

2 Put a spoonful of the filling toward the edge of a crepe. Fold the sides over it and roll up, as if wrapping a package. Continue until all the crepes and filling are used. Carefully dip each crepe in beaten egg, then into the cornmeal, to coat completely. Put the coated crepes on a piece of nonstick parchment paper and chill until required.

3 To make the sauce, mix all the ingredients in a small saucepan and simmer over moderate heat for 4–5 minutes, until glossy and syrupy. Pour into a pitcher to serve.

4 Heat the canola oil or peanut oil in a wok to 350–375°F, or until a cube of bread browns in 30 seconds. Add the crepes and deep-fry until crisp and golden brown. Drain on paper towels. To serve, pour a little sauce on each plate, add 1 or 2 crepes, and garnish with a red Swiss chard leaf.

Individual pea, spinach & mint pithiviers

SERVES 4
PREPARATION 25 MINUTES
COOKING 30 MINUTES

2 (5 oz) packages baby spinach leaves
1⅓ cups frozen peas, thawed
¼ cup chopped mint
12 oz frozen ready-to-bake all-butter
   puff pastry (see page 295)
1 cup garlic and herb cream cheese
¼ cup cream, to glaze
salt and black pepper

1 Wash the spinach, then place in a large saucepan with just the water clinging to the leaves and cook over high heat for 1–2 minutes, until wilted, then drain and cool. Season with salt and black pepper. Mash the peas with the mint—give them a quick blend in a food processor or with an immersion blender—so they hold together a little.

2 Lay the pastry on a board and roll to make it even thinner, then cut into four 4 inch circles for the bottoms, and 4 slightly larger ones, about 6¾ inches (a saucer is useful for cutting around), to go over the top.

3 Place the smaller circles on a baking sheet. Put a layer of spinach on top of each circle, leaving about ½ inch free around the edges. Put one-quarter of the garlic and herb cream cheese on top of the spinach, then pile the peas on top and around the garlic and herb cream cheese. Cover with the remaining pastry circles, pressing the edges neatly together and crimping with your fingers or the prongs of a fork. Make a hole in the center of each and decorate the top with little cuts spiraling out from the center, like traditional pithiviers, if you desire. All this can be done in advance. When ready to cook, brush the tops with the cream.

4 Bake the pithiviers in a preheated oven, at 400°F, for about 25 minutes, or until puffed up, golden brown, and crisp. Serve at once.

Sweet potato & wild rice patties with lime salsa •

I love the contrast between the bitter greens and the sweet patties—if you can't get kale, you can use spinach instead.

SERVES 6
PREPARATION 30 MINUTES
COOKING 1¼ HOURS

6 large sweet potatoes
1½ cups mixed basmati rice or other long-grain rice and wild rice
6–8 scallions, chopped
2 tablespoons grated fresh ginger root
8 garlic cloves, crushed
1½ cups cashew nuts, grated
cornmeal, for coating
olive oil, for pan-frying
salt and black pepper
kale or spinach, to serve

FOR THE SALSA

pared zest and chopped flesh of 1 lime
¼ cup chopped cilantro leaves
1 tablespoon dried coconut
1 green chile, seeded and chopped

1 Make a cut in the sweet potatoes to let out the steam, place them on a baking sheet, and bake in a preheated oven, at 450°F, for 50–60 minutes, or until they feel tender to the point of a knife. Remove from the oven and let cool a little. This can be done in advance if convenient.

2 Meanwhile, cook the rice. Bring a large saucepan of water to a boil. Add the rice, bring back to a boil, then reduce the heat and let simmer for 15–20 minutes, or according to the package directions, until the rice is tender. It can be a little on the soft side for this recipe. Drain into a colander, rinse under cold water, drain again, and put into a bowl.

3 Scoop the sweet potato flesh out of the skins and add to the rice, along with the scallions, ginger, garlic, and cashews. Season with salt and black pepper.

4 Form the mixture into 12 flat patties and coat with cornmeal, then set aside until required.

5 To make the salsa, simply mix all the ingredients together and set aside.

6 Just before you want to serve the meal, pour enough olive oil into a skillet to coat the bottom lightly. Heat until smoking, then add some of the patties. Cook until browned and crisp on one side, then turn them over and cook the other side, adding a little more olive oil as necessary. Lift them out carefully and put onto a baking sheet lined with paper towels. Keep them warm in the oven while you cook the rest.

7 Bring a 1 inch depth of water to a boil in a saucepan. Add the kale or spinach, then bring back to a boil, cover, and cook for 6–7 minutes, or until tender. Drain, then season with salt and black pepper.

8 Top each patty with a little of the salsa and serve with the greens—either all spread out on a large plate, the patties on top of the greens, or on individual plates.

Tofu braised with herbs & red wine ⓥ

Braising tofu in traditional French style is a great way to pack it with flavor and delectable juices. It's wonderful with creamy potatoes and a lightly cooked green vegetable or salad.

SERVES 4
PREPARATION 10 MINUTES,
   PLUS MARINATING
COOKING 45 MINUTES

2 x (8 oz) blocks firm tofu, drained
4 tablespoons ketjap manis (see page 294) or soy sauce
2–3 tablespoons olive oil
2 onions, sliced into rounds
2 carrots, sliced into thin sticks
7 oz turnips, diced
2 garlic cloves, finely chopped
2 tablespoons brandy
¼ pint red wine
¾ pint vegetable stock
small bunch of thyme
1 teaspoon sugar
salt and black pepper
chopped parsley, to garnish

1 Cut the tofu in half, then cut each slice in half widthwise, to make 8 "steaks." Lay these on a large shallow plate or container and pour over the ketjap manis or soy sauce, turning the pieces of tofu so that they are coated all over. Let marinate for 30 minutes.

2 Drain the tofu, reserving the liquid. Heat 2 tablespoons of the olive oil in a large shallow skillet or sauté pan, add the tofu and fry on both sides until well browned. Remove from the pan, add another tablespoon of olive oil, if necessary, and add the onions, carrots, and turnips. Fry for 10 minutes, browning lightly.

3 Add the tofu and its reserved liquid and the garlic to the pan with the brandy, wine, stock, thyme, sugar to taste, and some salt and black pepper.

4 Let the mixture simmer gently for about 30 minutes, or until all the vegetables are meltingly tender and bathed in a syrupy glaze. Serve from the pan, topped with a little chopped parsley.

Alfresco

Toasted Camembert open baguettes with shallots, thyme & red currants

If you prefer, use good-quality red currant jelly (or cranberry sauce) instead of the red currant mixture.

SERVES 4
PREPARATION 20 MINUTES
COOKING 30 MINUTES

2 tablespoons olive oil
1 cup sliced shallots
4 thyme sprigs
1 cup red currants
1 tablespoon water
⅔ cup granulated sugar
2 short baguettes
8 oz Camembert cheese,
   sliced with rind
leafy salad, to serve

1 Heat 1 tablespoon of the olive oil in a saucepan, add the shallots and thyme, cover, and cook gently for 10–15 minutes, until tender.

2 Meanwhile, to make the sauce, put the red currants into a saucepan with the water and cook for 2–3 minutes, until the juices run. Add the sugar, bring to a boil, and simmer for 5 minutes, then remove from the heat.

3 Split each baguette lengthwise, then cut each length in half, making 8 pieces of bread in all. Scoop out most of the soft crumb—this will not be needed.

4 Place the baguettes on a broiler pan. Put a layer of shallots, with the thyme sprigs, if you desire, into each baguette, then top with slices of Camembert. Put a little of the red currant mixture along the top—you won't need it all.

5 Brush the edges of each baguette with the remaining oil, then cook under a preheated broiler for 5–10 minutes, or until the bread has crisped and the Camembert has melted and become golden brown in places. Serve at once, with a leafy salad.

Spicy bean cakes with lemon mayonnaise

SERVES 4
PREPARATION 20 MINUTES
COOKING 30–35 MINUTES

1 tablespoon olive oil
1 onion, finely chopped
1 red bell pepper, cored, seeded,
   and chopped
2 garlic cloves, finely chopped
1 teaspoon cumin seeds
¼–½ teaspoon dried red pepper flakes
2 (15 oz) cans black beans or
   red kidney beans, well drained
¼ cup coarsely chopped cilantro
1 cup soft bread crumbs
a little cornmeal or dried
   bread crumbs, for coating
canola oil or light olive oil, for
   pan-frying
lemon wedges, to serve

FOR THE LEMON MAYONNAISE

1 egg
1 teaspoon Dijon mustard
1 tablespoon lemon juice
1¼ cups extra-light olive oil
   or other neutral-tasting oil
salt and black pepper

1 To make the mayonnaise, put the egg, mustard, lemon juice, and salt and black pepper into a food processor or blender and process for a few seconds to blend. Then, with the motor running, slowly pour in the oil through the hole in the top of the mixer, barely a trickle at first, increasing as the mayonnaise thickens. It will be thick when you have added all the oil. Check the seasoning and set aside.

2 To make the bean cakes, heat the olive oil in a saucepan, add the onion, cover, and cook for 5 minutes. Add the red bell pepper and garlic, stir, cover, and cook for another 10–15 minutes, until the vegetables are tender. Stir in the cumin seeds and red pepper flakes, cook for a minute or two longer, then remove from the heat.

3 Add the beans to the onion mixture, breaking them up with a potato masher, or process them briefly in a food processor until they are coarsely mashed—it's nice to have some big pieces. Add the cilantro, then stir in 2 tablespoons of the lemon mayonnaise and soft bread crumbs to make a soft mixture that holds together. Season with salt and black pepper.

4 Divide the mixture into 8 equal pieces, dip into cornmeal or dried bread crumbs and form into patty shapes. Heat a little canola oil or olive oil in a skillet and cook the bean cakes on both sides for 2–3 minutes until crisp. Drain on paper towels, then serve with the remaining lemon mayonnaise and some lemon wedges.

Eggplant steaks with mint glaze ⓥ

So simple—and so delicious—this has become one of my favorite ways to cook eggplant.

SERVES 4
PREPARATION 10 MINUTES,
 PLUS MARINATING
COOKING 20 MINUTES

2 large eggplants, stems trimmed
juice of 1 lime
2 tablespoons toasted sesame oil
2 tablespoons honey or maple syrup
¼ cup chopped mint

1 Cut each eggplant lengthwise into 4 thick slices. Cut crosshatching marks on both surfaces of the slices—on 2 of them you will be cutting the skin. Place the eggplant slices on a shallow pan or broiler pan.

2 Mix the lime juice with the sesame oil and honey or maple syrup. Drizzle the marinade over the surfaces of the eggplant, turning them over to drench both sides. Let marinate for 30 minutes, or up to 8 hours.

3 Cook the eggplant slices under a preheated hot broiler or on a barbecue until browned on one side, then turn them over and cook the other side until both sides are tender and lightly browned; this will take about 20 minutes.

4 Sprinkle with the chopped mint and serve immediately.

Haloumi with lime vinaigrette & mint in toasted mini pita

This has a great fresh taste and can be prepared in advance. I find it a particularly useful standby for unexpected visitors because it's easy to make and packages of haloumi (available in gourmet food stores and online) keep for a long time in the refrigerator.

SERVES 4
PREPARATION 10 MINUTES
COOKING 10 MINUTES

grated zest and juice of 2 limes
¼ cup olive oil
1 lb haloumi cheese or
    Muenster cheese
8 mini pita breads
leaves from 1 bunch of mint,
    coarsely chopped
½ cucumber, thinly sliced lengthwise
salt and black pepper

1 First make a lime vinaigrette by whisking together the zest and juice of the limes, the olive oil, and some black pepper—don't add any salt at this point because the haloumi cheese may supply enough. Set aside.

2 Drain off any water from the haloumi and blot the cheese with paper towels, if necessary. Cut the haloumi into slices about ¼ inch thick and put them in a single layer in a dry skillet. Cook over moderate-to-hot heat until they are browned on one side—this will take only a minute or two—then flip them over and cook the other side.

3 Meanwhile, toast the pita breads under a preheated broiler.

4 Remove the slices of haloumi from the pan when cooked and arrange them in a shallow serving dish. Pour the lime vinaigrette over the cheese and sprinkle with the mint, making sure that each slice gets coated. Serve with the toasted pita and sliced cucumber.

Chunky smoked cheese & parsley sausages

MAKES 12
PREPARATION 10 MINUTES
COOKING 5 MINUTES

10 oz Bavarian smoked cheese or
    other smoked cheese, shredded
    (about 3 cups)
4 cups soft whole-wheat bread crumbs
⅓ cup chopped parsley
2 shallots
olive oil, for pan-frying or brushing
salt and black pepper
hot pepper sauce, to serve

1 Put the smoked cheese, bread crumbs, parsley, shallots, and a little salt
and black pepper into a food processor and process to a smooth mixture
that holds together. Form into 12 fat chunky link sausage shapes.

2 Heat a little olive oil in a skillet and cook the sausages for 5 minutes, or
brush all over with olive oil and cook on a barbecue, turning them so
that they become crisp and golden brown all over.

3 Serve at once with hot pepper sauce, while they are hot and crisp on the
outside, melting and tender within.

Sage, onion & apple sausages

You can cook these sausages under a hot broiler or on a barbecue; or you can pan-fry them if you prefer.

SERVES 4
PREPARATION 15 MINUTES
COOKING 20 MINUTES

2 tablespoons olive oil, plus extra
  for brushing
2 onions, chopped
4 oz stale white bread, torn into
  chunks
10–12 sage leaves
4 oz cheddar cheese, broken into
  coarse chunks
1 Pippin or other sweet, crisp apple,
  peeled, cored, and cut into chunks
salt and black pepper

1 Heat the olive oil in a skillet, add the onions, and sauté for 10 minutes, until soft, then put them into a food processor with the bread, sage, cheddar, apple, and some salt and black pepper to taste. Blend until everything is chopped and starts to combine.

2 Check the seasoning, adding more salt and particularly black pepper, if required. Divide the mixture into 12 pieces and form each into a fat link sausage shape, pressing the mixture together well.

3 Brush the "sausages" with oil and broil, cook on a barbecue, or pan-fry them in a little oil, turning them so that they become golden brown all over. Drain on paper towels and eat while hot.

Polenta slices with roasted tomatoes

You can vary the flavoring for the polenta, which is Italian-style cornmeal. Try using chopped, pitted ripe black olives or green olives instead of the cheese or just plenty of chopped thyme and oregano.

SERVES 4
PREPARATION 15 MINUTES,
   PLUS COOLING
COOKING 50–60 MINUTES

5 cups water
2 cups instant polenta or regular
   cornmeal
1 cup grated Parmesan-style cheese or
   mature cheddar cheese
olive oil, for greasing and brushing
salt and black pepper

FOR THE ROASTED TOMATOES

2¼ lb small tomatoes on the vine
2 tablespoons olive oil
2 tablespoons balsamic vinegar
8–10 thyme sprigs

1 To make the polenta, bring the water to a boil in a large saucepan. Add the polenta to the water in a thin steady stream, stirring all the time. Let it simmer according to the package directions, stirring from time to time, until it's thick and leaves the sides of the pan. Alternatively, follow the package directions for making the cornmeal.

2 Remove from the heat and stir in the Parmesan or cheddar and season with salt and black pepper to taste. Transfer the mixture to a lightly oiled baking sheet or large plate, spreading and pressing it out to a depth of ¼–½ inch. Let stand until completely cold and firm.

3 To roast the tomatoes, put them, complete with their vines, into a roasting pan. Drizzle with the olive oil and vinegar, sprinkle with a little salt and the thyme sprigs, and place in the top of a preheated oven, at 400°F, for 40–45 minutes.

4 Just before you want to serve the meal, cut the polenta into slices, brush lightly with olive oil, and cook under a preheated broiler on both sides, until crisp and lightly charred. Serve at once, with the tomatoes.

Plantain bhajis with fresh coconut chutney ⓥ

SERVES 4 (MAKES ABOUT 20 BHAJIS)
PREPARATION 20 MINUTES
COOKING 15 MINUTES

1⅓ cups chickpea (besan) flour
½–1 teaspoon dried red pepper flakes
½ teaspoon turmeric
2 teaspoons ground coriander
2 teaspoons ground cumin
2 teaspoons cumin seeds
⅔–1 cup sparkling water
canola oil or peanut oil, for pan-frying
1 plantain
salt

FOR THE COCONUT CHUTNEY

1 cup freshly grated coconut
    (about ¼ of a coconut)
½ cup fresh cilantro
juice and grated zest of 1 lime
1 teaspoon black mustard seeds

1 First make the chutney. Put the grated coconut, fresh cilantro, and lime juice and zest into a food processor and process until combined. Stir in the mustard seeds and, if necessary, a little water to make a soft, creamy consistency. Set aside.

2 To make a batter, mix the chickpea flour, red pepper flakes, turmeric, ground coriander, ground and whole cumin seeds, and some salt with enough sparkling water to make a batter that will coat the back of the spoon.

3 When you are ready to serve the bhajis, heat 1 inch of canola oil or peanut oil in a skillet. Peel the plantain and cut it diagonally into slices about 1 inch thick.

4 Dip a slice of plantain into the batter, then put into the hot oil—it should sizzle immediately. Repeat with several more slices until the skillet is full. Turn the slices over when the underside is golden brown and crisp and cook on the other side. Drain on crumpled paper towels. Serve at once in batches, with the chutney—or keep the first ones warm while you fry the rest, then serve all at once, hot and crisp.

Zucchini & corn cakes with chili sauce ⓥ

Because these little corn cakes hold together so well, you could also cook them on a barbecue instead of frying them.

SERVES 4
PREPARATION 15 MINUTES
COOKING 15 MINUTES

2 tablespoons olive oil, plus extra
    for pan-frying
18 baby corn, sliced into ¼ inch circles
3½ cups shredded zucchini
3 garlic cloves, crushed
⅓ cup masa harina (see page 295)
1 teaspoon ground cumin
1 teaspoon dried dill weed
salt and black pepper
3 tablespoons chopped cilantro,
    to garnish
red chili sauce, to serve

1 Heat the 2 tablespoons of olive oil in a large saucepan, add the corn, zucchini, and garlic, and cook gently, stirring often, for about 5 minutes, until the vegetables are tender.

2 Add the masa harina, cumin, dill, and some salt and black pepper and stir well over the heat for 2–3 minutes, until the mixture is thick and holds together well. Leave until cool enough to handle, then form into 2 inch round cakes. You should make about 12–14.

3 Heat a little olive oil in a skillet and cook the cakes on both sides until golden brown and crisp. Drain on paper towels.

4 Transfer to a serving dish, sprinkle with the chopped cilantro, and serve immediately with red chili sauce for dipping.

Mexican tart with cumin pastry

This dramatic-looking tart has a hot and spicy red filling topped with eggs. To help the eggs set neatly, use fresh eggs.

SERVES 4
PREPARATION 30 MINUTES
COOKING 1 HOUR

2 cups all-purpose white flour
2 teaspoons cumin seeds
1 stick butter, cut into coarse
    chunks, plus extra for greasing
about ¼ cup cold water

FOR THE FILLING

2 onions, chopped
2 green bell peppers, cored, seeded,
    and chopped
1 tablespoon olive oil
2 (14½ oz) cans diced tomatoes
½ teaspoon dried red pepper flakes
5 particularly fresh eggs
salt and black pepper

1 To make the pastry, put the flour and cumin seeds into a bowl, add the butter, and rub in with your fingertips until the mixture resembles fine bread crumbs. Add enough cold water—3–4 tablespoons—to mix to a malleable dough.

2 Turn out the dough onto a lightly floured surface. Knead briefly, then roll out to fit a deep, greased 12 inch round tart pan. Trim the edges, prick the bottom, then cover it with nonstick parchment paper and some dried beans to weigh down the pastry.

3 Bake the tart shell in a preheated oven, at 400°F, for 20 minutes, until "set" and crisp. Remove the paper and beans and bake the tart shell for another 10 minutes, until the bottom is crisp. Remove the shell from the oven and reduce the oven temperature to 350°F.

4 Meanwhile, make the filling. Cook the onions and green bell peppers in the olive oil, covered, for 5 minutes, until beginning to get tender, then add the tomatoes and red pepper flakes and simmer, uncovered, over moderate heat for 25–30 minutes, or until thick, stirring from time to time to prevent it from sticking. Remove from the heat and season with salt and black pepper.

5 Spoon the tomato filling evenly into the pastry shell. Make a depression in the center, for 1 of the eggs, and 4 more evenly spaced around the edge. Break the eggs into the depressions and season lightly.

6 Cover the tart with aluminum foil, return to the oven, and bake for about 20 minutes, or until the eggs are set.

Potato & white truffle torte

This has a wonderful rich and seductive flavor. White truffle is fantastic in this if available, but you can also make a good version using Porcini and White Truffle Paste. It's very rich and great with a refreshing green salad.

SERVES 4
PREPARATION 20 MINUTES
COOKING 30 MINUTES

8 red-skinned or white round potatoes,
    peeled and cut into ¼ inch slices
2 garlic cloves, crushed
3 tablespoons butter, softened
2 oz white truffle, wiped, or
    3¼ oz jar porcini mushrooms
    in a vegetarian white truffle paste
    (see page 295)
2 cups grated Parmesan-style cheese
salt and black pepper
flat leaf parsley, to garnish

1 Put the potatoes into a saucepan, cover with water, and bring to a boil. Boil for about 10 minutes, or until tender but not soft. Drain.

2 Mix the garlic with the butter and use half to grease generously a 9–10 inch springform pan. Arrange a layer of potato in the pan, then grate some of the truffle over the top, or spread some truffle paste over the potatoes. Sprinkle with Parmesan and season with salt and black pepper.

3 Continue these layers, seasoning with salt and black pepper between each layer, until you have used all the ingredients, ending with a layer of potato and one of cheese. Dot with the remaining butter.

4 Bake in a preheated oven, at 450°F, for about 20 minutes, or until golden brown and crisp on top.

5 Remove the sides of the pan, slide the torte (on its bottom) onto a warmed plate, snip some parsley over the top, and serve immediately.

Dough ball, haloumi & olive skewers

The dough balls are quick and easy to make, but, if you prefer, you can make them ahead of time and freeze them, then thaw before using. You need 8 skewers for this recipe—if you use wooden ones, soak them in cold water for 10 minutes before use to prevent them from burning.

SERVES 4
PREPARATION 20 MINUTES,
   PLUS RISING
COOKING 10–15 MINUTES

2 (8 oz) packages haloumi cheese, drained, or Muenster or mozzarella cheese
24 large green olives, pitted
olive oil, for brushing

FOR THE DOUGH BALLS

2 cups white bread flour
1¼ teaspoons active dry yeast
1 teaspoon salt
¾ cup warm water
2 tablespoons olive oil

FOR THE LEMON BUTTER

juice and grated zest of ½ lemon
1 stick butter, softened

1 To make the dough balls, put the flour into a food processor fitted with a plastic dough blade. Add the yeast, salt, water, and olive oil and pulse until a dough forms, then blend for 1 minute. Let rest, with the lid on, for 45 minutes, or until the dough has doubled in size.

2 Divide the dough into 24 equal pieces and roll into marble-size balls.

3 Cut each block of haloumi into 12 cubes. Thread a dough ball onto a skewer followed by an olive and a cube of haloumi; repeat twice so that each skewer contains 3 each of dough balls, cheese cubes, and olives. Brush lightly with olive oil and place on a broiler pan or baking sheet. When all the skewers are done, cover them with a piece of plastic wrap or a clean damp cloth and let rest for 50–60 minutes for the dough balls to rise.

4 These skewers can be cooked in the oven, at 400°F, under the broiler, or on a barbecue. Preheat the cooking appliance in advance, then cook the skewers, turning them when the first side is done. They will take about 5 minutes on each side.

5 To make the lemon butter, beat the lemon juice and zest into the butter and serve with the dough ball skewers.

Egg-stuffed tomatoes with garlic & basil

SERVES 4
PREPARATION 10 MINUTES
COOKING 15 MINUTES

4 beefsteak tomatoes
2 tablespoons milk or cream
8 eggs, beaten
4 tablespoons butter
1 garlic clove, crushed
8 large basil leaves, shredded
salt and black pepper
buttered whole-grain toast, to serve

1 Cut the tomatoes in half horizontally and scoop out the seeds and pulp with a teaspoon. You won't need them for this recipe, but could add them to a soup or casserole—or just eat them!

2 Season the insides of the tomatoes with salt and black pepper and put them, cut side up, in a shallow gratin dish that will fit under your broiler and that you can later take to the table. Cook under a preheated broiler for about 10 minutes, or until tender, but not collapsed.

3 Just before the tomatoes are ready, make the scrambled eggs. Whisk the milk or cream into the beaten eggs and season with salt and black pepper.

4 Cut half the butter into tiny pieces and set aside. Melt the remaining butter in a saucepan, add the garlic, and cook for a few seconds, but don't let the butter or garlic brown.

5 Pour in the eggs and stir over gentle heat until the eggs begin to thicken and scramble. As soon as this starts to happen, stir in the remaining butter and the basil and remove the pan from the heat—the eggs will continue to cook in the residual heat.

6 Spoon the scrambled egg into the tomato halves, dividing the mixture equally among them and serve immediately, with hot whole-grain toast.

Baby potatoes & mushrooms on rosemary skewers

If you can't get "baby" potatoes, use ordinary new potatoes halved; and instead of rosemary sprigs, you could use wooden skewers.

SERVES 4

PREPARATION 15 MINUTES

COOKING 25 MINUTES

18 baby potatoes

6 rosemary sprigs, 10–12 inches long

18 baby cremini mushrooms

2–3 tablespoons olive oil

sea salt flakes

lemon mayonnaise (see page 160),
   peanut dip (see page 22), or red
   pepper hummus (see page 30),
   to serve

1 Put the potatoes into a saucepan, cover with water, and bring to a boil, then reduce the heat and simmer for 6–10 minutes, depending on the size of the potatoes, until they are just tender when pierced with the point of a knife. Drain and cool.

2 Using your fingers, pull off most of the leaves from the rosemary, leaving 3–4 inches at the top.

3 Thread the mushrooms and potatoes alternately onto the rosemary sprigs—they should go on easily. Brush all over with olive oil.

4 Cook the skewers on a preheated barbecue or under a preheated hot broiler, keeping the leafy ends away from the heat, for about 15 minutes, until the potatoes are golden brown and the mushrooms tender. Sprinkle with sea salt and serve with lemon mayonnaise, peanut dip, or red pepper hummus.

Crispy nut balls coated in cornmeal

The nut mixture is molded around a piece of garlic butter, providing a gorgeous burst of flavor as you bite into each ball. They're nice served with toothpicks and dipped into a sauce—either mayonnaise, if you feel like something rich and creamy, or a Japanese-style soy sauce dip for a clean, savory flavor.

MAKES 24
PREPARATION 20 MINUTES,
   PLUS COOLING
COOKING 20 MINUTES

6 tablespoons butter, softened
2 garlic cloves, crushed
1 small onion, finely chopped
3 tablespoons whole-wheat flour
1 cup soy milk
2 teaspoons chopped oregano
½ cup hazelnuts, finely ground
1 egg, beaten
cornmeal, for coating
canola oil, for deep-frying
salt and black pepper
lemon wedges, to serve

FOR THE SOY SAUCE DIP

2 tablespoons soy sauce
2 tablespoons mirin
2 tablespoons sake

1 To make the dip, mix together the soy sauce, mirin, and sake. Put it into a small serving bowl and set aside.

2 Beat 4 tablespoons of the butter with the garlic until light and creamy, then form into a small block, wrap in aluminum foil, and put into the refrigerator to chill and harden—this can be done well in advance, if convenient.

3 Next, make the nut mixture, which needs to be done in advance, so it can cool before use. Melt the remaining butter in a large saucepan, add the onion, cover, and sauté gently for about 7 minutes, until tender. Stir in the whole-wheat flour and cook for 2–3 minutes, but don't let it brown, then pour in the soy milk and stir over the heat until thick. Remove from the heat, stir in the oregano, ground hazelnuts, and salt and black pepper to taste. Spread out on a plate and let stand until completely cold.

4 Divide the firm garlic butter into 24 pieces. Take a heaping teaspoon of the nut mixture, form it into a small ball, then push a piece of garlic butter into the center and cover over with the nut mixture. Dip into the beaten egg, then into the cornmeal. Continue until you've used all the butter and nut mixture and made 24 balls.

5 Heat the canola oil in a wok to 350°F, or until a cube of bread browns in 30 seconds. Add the nut balls, a few at a time, and deep-fry for a minute or two until golden brown and crisp. Drain on paper towels.

6 Put the nut balls on a serving plate and serve with the bowl of soy sauce dip, or just as they are with toothpicks, mayonnaise, and lemon wedges.

Cheese & sun-dried tomato muffins

Everyone enjoys these light, puffy, protein-rich savory muffins—and because they don't contain any wheat flour, they're ideal for people who are watching their carbohydrate intake.

MAKES 9
PREPARATION 10 MINUTES
COOKING 20 MINUTES

1 cup plain cottage cheese
¾ cup grated Parmesan-style cheese
½ cup soy flour
1 cup ground almonds (almond meal)
1 teaspoon baking powder
8 sun-dried tomato pieces,
   finely chopped
¼ cup chopped basil
¼ cup water
4 eggs
salt and black pepper

1 Line 9 sections in a cupcake pan with paper cupcake liners to make small muffins.

2 Put the cottage cheese into a bowl with all but 3 tablespoons of the Parmesan, the soy flour, ground almonds, baking powder, sun-dried tomatoes, basil, water, and eggs and season with salt and black pepper, then mix all together.

3 Spoon the batter into the paper liners, sprinkle with the remaining Parmesan, and bake in a preheated oven, at 400°F, for 20 minutes, or until set, risen, and golden brown. Serve as soon as possible—they're best eaten warm.

Honey corn muffins

MAKES 12
PREPARATION 20 MINUTES
COOKING 10–15 MINUTES

⅔ cup whole-wheat flour
⅔ cup cornmeal
2½ teaspoons baking powder
3 tablespoons sunflower seeds
2 eggs
¾ cup milk
⅓ cup honey
2 tablespoons olive oil

1 Line a 12-section muffin pan with 12 paper muffin liners.

2 Put the flour into a bowl with the cornmeal, baking powder, and half the sunflower seeds.

3 Whisk together the eggs, milk, honey, and olive oil, then stir quickly into the dry ingredients—don't mix it too much.

4 Divide the batter between the paper liners and sprinkle the remaining sunflower seeds on top of each muffin. Bake in a preheated oven, at 400°F, for 10–15 minutes, until risen, golden, and firm to a light touch. These muffins are delicious for breakfast straight from the oven, or can be reheated for a few minutes before serving.

Fruit fajita dessert

This sweet version of fajitas makes a fun help-yourself dessert, ideal for an informal meal with friends.

SERVES 4
PREPARATION 25 MINUTES
COOKING 15 MINUTES

FOR THE FAJITAS

1 cup all-purpose white flour
2 teaspoons granulated sugar
2 eggs
1¼ cups milk and water mixed
a little flavorless oil, such as
   peanut, for pan-frying

FOR THE FRUIT SALAD

2 ripe pears, peeled and cut into
   bite-size pieces
1 cup hulled small strawberries
1 cup halved purple or red seedless
   grapes
2 ripe kiwifruit, peeled and sliced
juice of 1 orange

TO SERVE

toasted almonds or coconut
whipped heavy cream
maple syrup
granulated sugar
slices of lime

1 All the preparation for this can be done in advance. First, make the fajitas, which are in fact sweet pancakes. Put the flour, sugar, eggs, and most of the milk and water into a blender or food processor and blend to a smooth batter, adding the rest of the liquid, if necessary, to make a consistency like light cream. Alternatively, sift the flour into a bowl, add the sugar, and break in the eggs. Beat together, adding the liquid gradually to make a smooth batter.

2 Heat 1 tablespoon of oil in a skillet. When it's hot, swirl the oil around the pan and tip any excess into a cup. Pour in a good 2 tablespoons of the batter and tilt the pan so that it spreads all over the bottom—you may need a little more or less batter, depending on the size of your skillet, but the pancakes need to be thick enough to be rolled around the fruit salad filling later—more robust than delicate crepes but not as thick as normal pancakes.

3 After a minute or so, when the top of the pancake has set, flip it over with a spatula and cook the other side, which will take only a few seconds. Put the pancake onto a plate and continue to make more in the same way, piling them up on the plate. Grease the skillet with more oil as required.

4 Make the fruit salad by mixing together all the fruits and adding the orange juice. Put into a serving bowl and keep cool.

5 Serve a pile of fajitas with the bowl of fruit salad and small bowls of toasted almonds or coconut, whipped heavy cream, maple syrup, granulated sugar, and lime slices for people to help themselves. Plenty of napkins and finger bowls might be a good idea.

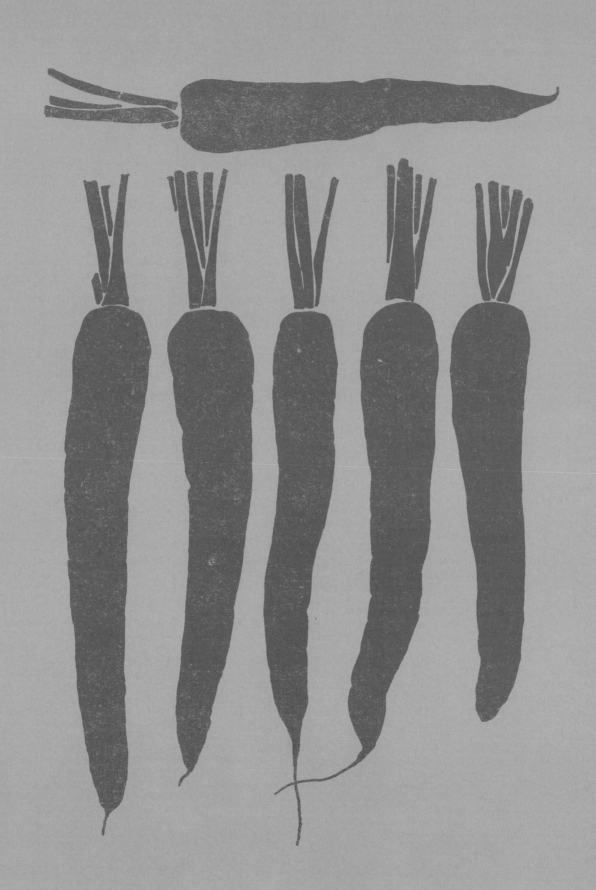

Parties & celebrations

Canapés: bruschette with three toppings

MAKES 24
PREPARATION 40 MINUTES
COOKING 30 MINUTES

1 baguette
olive oil
dried rosemary
salt and black pepper

FOR THE EGGPLANT CAVIAR

2 eggplants, stems trimmed
1–2 garlic cloves, crushed
2 tablespoons tahini
2 tablespoons olive oil
2 tablespoons lemon juice
paprika pepper and garlic sprouts,
   to garnish (optional)

FOR THE GOAT CHEESE WITH
RED ONION AND BEETS

1 tablespoon olive oil
2 red onions, thinly sliced
1 tablespoon granulated sugar
1 tablespoon red wine vinegar
3 cups diced cooked beets
7 oz soft goat cheese
rosemary leaves, to garnish

FOR THE CHESTNUT PÂTÉ

10 vacuum-packed or canned
   whole peeled chestnuts
1 tablespoon butter
1 garlic clove, crushed
2 tablespoons lemon juice
finely chopped sweet red peppers from
   a jar and thyme sprigs, to garnish

1 Start by making the bruschette. Slice the bread, then brush each slice on both sides with olive oil and sprinkle each piece on both sides with a good pinch of crushed rosemary. Place the bread on a baking sheet and bake in a preheated oven, at 300°F, for about 20 minutes, until crisp. Cool on wire racks. They can be made up to 1 week in advance and kept in an airtight container.

2 Next, make the toppings. For the eggplant caviar, prick the eggplants in several places, then cook them under a preheated hot broiler for 25–30 minutes, until soft and well charred. Cool slightly, then peel off the skin and put the eggplant into a food processor with the garlic, tahini, the 2 tablespoons olive oil, and the lemon juice and blend to a pale cream. Season with salt and black pepper and chill until required.

3 For the caramelized onion and beets, heat the olive oil in a large saucepan, add the onions, cover, and cook for about 15 minutes, until they're tender, stirring them every 5 minutes. Add the sugar, wine vinegar, and beets, then simmer gently, uncovered, for 10–15 minutes. Remove from the heat, season, and cool.

4 For the chestnut pâté, put the chestnuts into a food processor with the butter, garlic, and lemon juice. Blend to a fairly smooth puree and season with salt and black pepper.

5 To complete the bruschette, spread one-third of the bottoms with eggplant caviar and garnish with a drizzle of olive oil, a dusting of paprika pepper, and a few garlic sprouts, if desired. Spread another third of the bottoms with goat cheese, top with the caramelized onion and beets, and a piece of rosemary. Spread the remaining bruschette with chestnut pâté and garnish with sweet red peppers and thyme sprigs.

Mini carrot & cardamom tarte tatins

With their crisp flaky pastry crusts and glossy orange tops of tender, melting carrot, these are gorgeous and not difficult to make.

MAKES 16
PREPARATION 25 MINUTES,
    PLUS COOLING
COOKING 35 MINUTES

10 carrots (about 1½ lb), thinly sliced
1 large garlic clove, crushed
3 tablespoons olive oil
¾ cup water
1½ teaspoons granulated sugar
20 cardamom pods
12 oz frozen ready-to-bake all-butter
    puff pastry (see page 295)
salt and black pepper

1 Put the sliced carrots into a saucepan with the garlic, olive oil, water, sugar, and some salt and black pepper.

2 Crush the cardamom and discard the pods. Crush the seeds a little, then add to the saucepan. Bring to a boil, then reduce the heat, cover, and cook gently for about 10 minutes, or until the carrots are tender and glossy, and the water has disappeared. If there is still water left, remove the lid from the pan and boil the liquid rapidly until it has disappeared. Cool.

3 Line an 8½ x 12½ inch jellyroll pan with nonstick parchment paper. Spread the carrots evenly over the bottom and cover with the pastry, pressing it down and trimming it to fit. Prick the pastry all over, then bake in a preheated oven, at 400°F, for 15 minutes, until puffy, golden brown, and crisp.

4 Let the tart cool completely, then turn it out onto a board so that the carrots are on top. Using a 1½ inch plain round cutter, carefully cut out 16 circles. You may need to use a sharp knife in addition to the cutter to get through the pastry.

5 Just before serving, put the little tarte tatins onto an ovenproof serving dish and put into the oven for a few minutes to warm through.

Mini watercress roulade slices

These are really easy to do, and they look and taste impressive.

MAKES 18
PREPARATION 25 MINUTES
COOKING 15 MINUTES

2 tablespoons butter
1 (5 oz) package watercress or arugula,
   finely chopped
3 eggs
⅔ cup garlic and herb cream cheese
salt and black pepper

1 Melt the butter in a saucepan, add the watercress or arugula, and cook over moderate heat for about 3 minutes, or until the greens have wilted.

2 Puree the greens in a food processor, then add the eggs and some salt and black pepper and blend until combined.

3 Line an 8½ x 12½ inch jellyroll pan with nonstick parchment paper. Pour the mixture into the pan, making sure it flows into the corners. Bake in a preheated oven, at 400°F, for about 12 minutes, or until set. Remove from the oven and let cool.

4 Turn out the roulade onto a piece of nonstick parchment paper and strip off the backing paper.

5 Beat the cream cheese in a bowl until soft, adding 1–2 tablespoons of hot water, if necessary, then spread evenly over the top of the roulade.

6 With the long side facing you, make an incision about ¼ inch in from the edge, but don't cut right through. Bend this piece of roulade up, pressing it against the filling, then continue to roll it firmly to make a small roulade, like a jellyroll. Wrap in nonstick parchment paper until required, then unwrap and cut into 18 little slices to serve.

Asian omelet wraps

MAKES 20
PREPARATION 30 MINUTES
COOKING 15 MINUTES

4 inch piece of cucumber, peeled
4 scallions
1 tablespoon rice vinegar
1 tablespoon shoyu or tamari
1 tablespoon mirin
4 eggs
toasted sesame oil, for frying
salt and black pepper

TO GARNISH

sesame seeds
radish roses
scallion tassels

1 Cut the cucumber and scallions into matchsticks about 2 inches long. Put them into a shallow dish and add the rice vinegar, shoyu or tamari, and the mirin, then mix gently and set aside.

2 Beat the eggs with some salt and black pepper. Coat a skillet thinly with sesame oil and heat.

3 Pour about 1 tablespoon of the beaten egg into the skillet. Let it run a little, but tilt the skillet so that the omelet stays as round as possible. When the top has set completely, lift the omelet from the pan with a spatula, roll it up lightly, and put it on a plate. Continue making another 19 omelets in the same way, until all the egg has been used.

4 Unroll one of the omelets, put a few matchsticks of cucumber and one of scallion in the center and reroll it. Place on a serving dish, seam side down. Make the rest in the same way, arranging them all around the edge of a plate, like the spokes of a wheel.

5 Sprinkle the omelets with a few sesame seeds and put some radish roses and scallion tassels in the center of the plate to garnish. Keep cool until required.

Tiny tortillas

These are delectable as they are, garnished with a spoonful of chive sour cream, or served with a bowl of sour cream and chives for dipping.

MAKES 20
PREPARATION 15 MINUTES
COOKING 30 MINUTES

4 red-skinnned or white round
  potatoes, peeled and cut
  into even pieces
4 scallions, chopped
1 red bell pepper, cored, seeded, and
  finely chopped
2 eggs, beaten
olive oil, for pan-frying
½ cup shredded vegetarian Gruyère
  cheese or similar cheese, such as
  Swiss or Gouda
5–6 cherry tomatoes, sliced
salt and black pepper
⅔ cup sour cream and 2 tablespoons
  chopped chives, to garnish (optional)

1 Put the potatoes into a saucepan, cover with boiling water, and cook for about 10 minutes, until they are just tender. Drain and cool.

2 Cut the potatoes into small cubes—about 1 inch—then mix with the scallions, red bell pepper, eggs, and some salt and black pepper.

3 Heat a little olive oil in a skillet. Put tablespoons of the tortilla mixture into the hot oil, forming them into circles, and cook gently for about 5 minutes, or until the bottoms of the tortillas are golden brown and the tops have more or less set. Drain on a plate lined with paper towels and keep cool until you want to serve them.

4 Place the tortillas, in a single layer, on a flat ovenproof plate. Top each tortilla with a little cheese and a slice of tomato, then put them under a preheated hot broiler or into a hot oven for about 5 minutes, or until they are heated through and the tops are golden brown. Garnish each with a teaspoon of sour cream and some chopped chives, if desired, and serve immediately.

Mini feta & sun-dried tomato muffins

MAKES 30
PREPARATION 10 MINUTES
COOKING 10 MINUTES

2 tablespoons olive oil, plus extra
   for greasing
1 egg
2 tablespoons tomato paste
2 tablespoons water
1 cup all-purpose white flour
2 teaspoons baking powder
7 oz feta cheese, cut into tiny dice
8 sun-dried tomatoes in oil, drained
   and finely chopped
¼ cup lightly chopped basil
salt and black pepper

1 Line the bottoms of a 12-section mini-muffin pan, each hole measuring ¾ inch across and about ¾ inch deep, with circles of nonstick parchment paper, then brush them with olive oil. Alternatively, line the pan with mini paper liners if you have them.

2 Beat together the 2 tablespoons olive oil, the egg, tomato paste, and water.

3 Sift together the flour and baking powder into a bowl, then mix in the feta, sun-dried tomatoes, basil, and some salt and black pepper. Make a well in the center and add the egg mixture. Stir until just combined; do not overmix.

4 Spoon into the prepared mini-muffin sections or liners, filling them well, and bake in a preheated oven, at 375°F, for about 8 minutes, or until golden brown.

5 Remove from the oven and let stand for 5 minutes to settle, then slip them out of the pan with a knife and let cool on a wire rack.

6 The muffins can be reheated before serving. Put them on an ovenproof plate and put into a preheated oven, at 350°F, for about 5 minutes, to heat through and puff up.

Pecorino bites

MAKES 12
PREPARATION 20 MINUTES
COOKING 20 MINUTES

4 russet or Yukon gold potatoes, peeled
    and cut into even pieces
2 tablespoons truffle oil
¼ cup grated vegetarian Pecorino
    cheese or Parmesan-style cheese
1–2 teaspoons porcini in a vegetarian
    white truffle paste (see page 295)
1 extra-large egg, beaten
¼–⅓ cup dried bread crumbs
canola oil or peanut oil, for
    deep-frying
salt and black pepper

1 Put the potatoes into a saucepan, cover with boiling water, and cook for about 15 minutes, or until tender. Drain thoroughly. Mash the potatoes with the truffle oil, Pecorino, and some salt and black pepper. Let stand until cool enough to handle.

2 Divide the mixture into 12 equal portions. Flatten each piece, then put a small spoonful—about ⅛ teaspoon—of truffle paste onto the center of each. Take each of the circles, draw the sides up so that the truffle paste is enclosed, and form into a ball shape. Dip the balls first in the beaten egg and then in the dried bread crumbs, so that they are completely coated.

3 Heat the canola oil or peanut oil in a wok to 350–375°F, or until a cube of bread browns in 30 seconds. Add the potato balls and deep-fry for 2–3 minutes, or until golden and crisp. Drain on paper towels. Serve hot, warm, or cold.

Artichoke & green olive "cake" with sizzling pine nuts & saffron cream

You can buy marinated artichoke hearts from a deli or, for perfection, boil the bottoms of globe artichokes until tender, having first cut off all the leaves and removed the "chokes."

SERVES 6
PREPARATION 30 MINUTES
COOKING 1¼ HOURS

2 tablespoons butter, plus extra
    for greasing
1 tablespoon olive oil
1 lb new potatoes, cut into
    ⅛ inch slices
⅔ cup water
3 cups coarsely chopped cooked
    artichoke bottoms or marinated
    artichoke hearts
1½ cups pitted large green olives,
    coarsely chopped
¼ cup chopped parsley
1 cup soft white bread crumbs
4 eggs, beaten
⅔ cup light cream
salt and black pepper
flat leaf parsley, to garnish

FOR THE SAFFRON CREAM

1¼ cups heavy cream
½ teaspoon saffron threads

FOR THE TOPPING

2 tablespoons butter
1 tablespoon olive oil
4 garlic cloves, sliced
2 tablespoons pine nuts

1 Line a 9 x 5 x 3 inch loaf pan with a strip of nonstick parchment paper and grease with butter.

2 Heat the butter and olive oil in a saucepan, then add the potatoes and water. Bring to a boil, then reduce the heat, cover, and cook gently for 10–15 minutes, or until the potatoes are tender and most of the water has disappeared.

3 Mix together the potatoes and their cooking liquid, the artichokes, olives, parsley, bread crumbs, eggs, light cream, and salt and black pepper to taste. Spoon the mixture into the prepared loaf pan and level the surface. Bake in a preheated oven, at 350°F, for 1 hour, or until it is firm and a toothpick inserted into the center comes out clean.

4 To make the saffron cream, put the heavy cream and saffron into a saucepan, bring to a boil, then season with salt and black pepper. Let steep until ready to serve, then reheat.

5 Turn out the "cake" onto a warmed serving plate and keep warm while you make the pine nut topping. Heat the butter and olive oil in a saucepan and add the garlic and pine nuts. Cook over moderate heat for a minute or two until the pine nuts and garlic are golden brown, then remove from the heat and pour, sizzling, over the top of the cake. Garnish with some flat leaf parsley and serve immediately, with the saffron cream.

Baby popovers with nut roast & horseradish

These are fabulous, and not nearly as much work as you might think, because they can be prepared in advance and then just reheated before serving—they'll puff up beautifully.

MAKES 24
PREPARATION 20 MINUTES,
    PLUS STANDING
COOKING 35 MINUTES

⅓ cup all-purpose white flour
1 egg
⅓ cup milk
⅓ cup water
2 tablespoons olive oil, plus extra
    for greasing
salt and black pepper
horseradish sauce, to serve

FOR THE NUT ROAST

½ cup almonds
1 slice of whole-wheat bread
½ cup shredded cheese
⅓ cup coarsely chopped onion
½ teaspoon dried mixed herbs
1 tablespoon shoyu or tamari

1   Sift the flour into a bowl with a pinch of salt. Make a well in the center, break the egg into it, and mix to a paste, then gradually draw in the flour. Mix the milk with the water, then stir into the bowl, but don't overbeat. Transfer the batter to a small bowl, or preferably a liquid measuring cup so that it will be easy to pour into the pan, and let rest for 30 minutes. This allows for the starch to swell, producing a lighter result.

2   Meanwhile, make the nut roast. Put all the ingredients into a food processor and blend until you have a smooth mixture that holds together. Form it into 24 small link sausage shapes, coat all over with olive oil, and place on a baking sheet.

3   Use two 12-section nonstick mini-muffin pans, each section measuring ¾ inch across and about ¾ inch deep. Put ½ teaspoon olive oil into each section and put the pans into a preheated oven, at 425°F. The oil needs to heat for 10 minutes before you put the batter in.

4   Put the nut roast sausages in the oven at this point (they will take longer to cook than the popovers) and roast for about 15 minutes, or until they are brown and crisp.

5   When the oil in the muffin pans is smoking hot, quickly pour the batter into each section, filling it about two-thirds full. Bake for 10 minutes, until puffed up and golden. Remove the popovers from the pan and cool on a wire rack.

6   When you want to serve the popovers, put them on a heatproof serving dish and place a small piece of nut roast on top of each. Put them in the oven, at 425°F, for 4–5 minutes, until hot and puffy. Serve immediately with horseradish sauce.

Little fava bean & mint risottos

Creamy risotto, served piping hot in little ramekins with tiny spoons, makes a sensational party dish and is easy to do.

SERVES 24
PREPARATION 30 MINUTES
COOKING 30 MINUTES

2 cups frozen fava beans
4 cups vegetable stock
1 tablespoon olive oil
bunch of scallions, finely chopped
2 garlic cloves, finely chopped
2 cups risotto rice
3–4 large mint sprigs
½ cup dry white wine
4 tablespoons butter
1¼ cups grated Parmesan-style cheese
salt and black pepper
chopped mint, to garnish

1 Cook the fava beans in a saucepan of boiling water for 4–5 minutes, then drain and cool. Pop the bright green beans out of their gray skins and put to one side. Discard the skins.

2 To make the risotto, put the stock into a saucepan and bring to a boil, then reduce the heat and keep hot over gentle heat.

3 Heat the olive oil in a large saucepan, add the scallions, and stir, then cover and cook gently for 3–4 minutes, until tender but not browned. Stir in the garlic and cook for a minute or two longer.

4 Add the rice to the pan, along with the mint sprigs, and stir over gentle heat for 2–3 minutes, or until the rice looks translucent, then pour in the wine and stir all the time as it simmers away.

5 When the wine has disappeared, add a ladleful of the hot stock and stir over low-to-medium heat until the rice has absorbed the stock. Add another ladleful and continue in this way, adding the fava beans with the final ladleful of stock, for 15–20 minutes, until you've used all the stock, the rice is tender and has a creamy consistency.

6 Remove the sprigs of mint, add the butter and half the Parmesan, and season with salt and black pepper. Immediately transfer the risotto into warmed ramekins, sprinkle each with a little Parmesan and chopped mint, and serve immediately, each with a tiny spoon.

Wild mushroom roulade

SERVES 6
PREPARATION 20 MINUTES
COOKING 25 MINUTES

⅓ cup chopped flat leaf parsley
¾ cup low-fat cream cheese
1½ cups shredded vegetarian Gruyère
   cheese or similar cheese, such as
   Swiss or Gouda
4 eggs, separated
salt and black pepper
Tomato sauce (see page 117), to serve

FOR THE FILLING

1 tablespoon olive oil
1 lb mixed wild mushrooms
   or oyster mushrooms, wiped
4 garlic cloves, finely chopped
⅔ cup garlic and herb cream cheese
1–2 tablespoons hot water

1   Line a 9 x 13 inch jellyroll pan with nonstick parchment paper so that it extends about 2 inches on all sides.

2   Set aside half the parsley for the garnish. Put into a large bowl with the low-fat cheese, the Gruyère, and the egg yolks. Mix well and season with salt and black pepper.

3   In another bowl, whisk the egg whites until they stand in stiff peaks, then, using a large metal spoon, fold them lightly into the Gruyère mixture.

4   Pour the mixture into the prepared jellyroll pan, spreading it evenly into the corners. Bake in a preheated oven, at 400°F, for 12 minutes, or until firm, golden brown, and well risen.

5   While the roulade is cooking, make the filling. Heat the olive oil in a large saucepan, add the mushrooms and garlic, and sauté over high heat for 4–5 minutes, until the mushrooms are tender. You can assemble the roulade at this point, or you can do it after the roulade has cooled when it can be a little easier to roll.

6   Put a large piece of nonstick parchment paper, a little bigger than the roulade, on the work surface and turn out the cooked roulade onto it. Strip off the backing paper.

7   Mix the garlic and herb cream cheese with enough hot water to soften it a little, then spread it evenly over the roulade. Arrange the mushrooms on top, taking them to within ½ inch of the short edges. Make sure any thick mushroom stems are parallel with the short edges; this makes it easier to roll them up. Now for the fun! Starting with one short end, fold up about ½ inch of the roulade and press it down firmly. Using the paper to help you and holding the folded end through the paper, start rolling firmly, like a jellyroll, then press the roulade into a good shape when it's rolled up.

8   Put the roulade, seam side down, onto a heatproof serving plate. Now either reheat it in the oven for 5–10 minutes, until piping hot, or let it cool and reheat it later for 10–15 minutes. It will puff up a little and smell divine.

9   Garnish the top with the reserved parsley and cut into thick slices to serve, with the tomato sauce.

Christmas tart

This tart is full of Christmas flavors. Serve it with roasted potatoes and cranberry sauce.

SERVES 6
PREPARATION 30 MINUTES,
    PLUS CHILLING
COOKING 30–35 MINUTES

3 cups whole-wheat flour
    or half whole-wheat, half white
1½ sticks butter, cut into
    coarse chunks
½ teaspoon salt
3 tablespoons cold water
2 tablespoons olive oil

FOR THE FILLING

6 carrots, cleaned and sliced
4 leeks, trimmed and cut into
    1 inch pieces
9 oz shallots
12 oz trimmed small Brussels sprouts
2 Pippin or other sweet, crisp apples,
    peeled, cored, and chopped
1 cup cashew nuts
salt and black pepper
chopped parsley, to garnish

FOR THE SAUCE

4 tablespoons butter
2 tablespoons cornstarch or arrowroot
1 cup soy milk
6 oz Stilton cheese or other
    blue cheese, crumbled

1   To make the pastry dough, put the flour, butter, and salt into a food processor and blend until it resembles coarse bread crumbs. Alternatively, put the ingredients into a bowl and rub the butter into the flour with your fingertips. Add the water and mix to a dough.

2   Turn out the dough onto a lightly floured surface. Knead briefly, then form into a circle and roll out to fit a round tart pan measuring 12 inches across and 1½ inches deep. Trim the edges, prick the bottom thoroughly all over, then chill for 30 minutes.

3   Bake the tart in a preheated oven, at 400°F, for 20 minutes, until the pastry is "set" and lightly browned. A minute or two before you take it out of the oven, heat the olive oil in a small saucepan until smoking hot. As soon as the tart comes out of the oven, pour the hot olive oil all over the bottom—it will sizzle and almost "fry." This will "waterproof" the bottom of the tart so that it will remain crisp.

4   Meanwhile, to make the filling, fill a large saucepan halfway with water and bring to a boil. Add the carrots, leeks, and shallots, bring back to a boil, cover, and cook for 5 minutes, then add the sprouts, cover, and cook for another 6–7 minutes, until all the vegetables are tender. Drain.

5   To make the sauce, melt the butter in a saucepan and stir in the cornstarch or arrowroot. When it froths at the edges, pour in the soy milk and stir over the heat until it has thickened. Remove from the heat and stir in the blue cheese. Season with salt and black pepper.

6   Mix the sauce with the drained vegetables and the apple. Check the seasoning, then spoon into the tart shell and top with the cashew nuts. Put back into the oven for 10–15 minutes, until the filling is piping hot and the cashew nuts are golden brown. Sprinkle with chopped parsley and serve immediately.

Moroccan-flavored eggplant Wellington ⓥ

SERVES 6
PREPARATION 20 MINUTES,
  PLUS COOLING
COOKING 1 HOUR

⅔ cup couscous
2 tablespoons olive oil
1 onion, chopped
1 eggplant, cut into ½ inch cubes
1 red bell pepper, cored, seeded, and
  cut into ½ inch pieces
3 tablespoons chopped dried apricots
3 tablespoons raisins
2 garlic cloves, crushed
1 tablespoon ground cinnamon
1 tablespoon ground cumin
1 tablespoon chopped mint
1 tablespoon chopped parsley
1 cup toasted slivered almonds
1 cup sliced, pitted ripe black olives
2 (12 oz) sheets of ready-to-bake
  puff pastry
soy milk, for brushing
sesame seeds, for sprinkling
salt and black pepper

1 Put the couscous into a bowl, cover the grains with boiling water, and let stand to soak.

2 Meanwhile, heat the olive oil in a large saucepan, add the onion, and sauté for 5 minutes, then add the eggplant and red bell pepper, cover, and cook gently for 10–15 minutes, or until the vegetables are tender. Add the apricots, raisins, garlic, cinnamon, and cumin and stir over the heat for a minute or two until the spices smell aromatic. Remove from the heat.

3 Drain the couscous thoroughly in a strainer and add it to the pan, along with the mint, parsley, almonds, and olives. Season with salt and black pepper to taste and let the mixture cool.

4 Spread a pastry sheet out on a baking sheet and brush with soy milk.

5 Put the eggplant mixture in the center of the pastry. Place the second sheet of pastry over the top and press the edges together. Trim the edges, leaving a 1 inch border. Pinch the edges with your fingers and thumbs. Brush with soy milk and sprinkle with sesame seeds.

6 Bake in a preheated oven, at 400°F, for 40 minutes, until the pastry has puffed up and is golden brown. Transfer to a warmed serving plate and serve immediately.

Luscious vegan pumpkin pie ⓥ

SERVES 6

PREPARATION 30 MINUTES,
  PLUS PUMPKIN BAKING

COOKING 40 MINUTES

2⅓ cups whole-wheat flour
  or half whole-wheat, half white
1¼ sticks vegan margarine or
  butter, cut into coarse chunks
½ teaspoon salt
2–3 tablespoons cold water
2–3 tablespoons soy milk
granulated sugar, for dredging
ground cinnamon, for sprinkling
vegan ice cream, soy cream, or yogurt,
  to serve

FOR THE FILLING

2 cups canned pumpkin puree or
  1 butternut squash
9 oz firm tofu, drained, patted
  dry, and broken into chunks
⅔ cup firmly packed brown sugar
1 tablespoon molasses
1 teaspoon ground cinnamon
½ teaspoon ground ginger
½ teaspoon grated nutmeg

1 If you are using fresh butternut squash, halve, seed, and place, cut side down, on a baking sheet. Bake in a preheated oven, at 400°F, for 40–60 minutes, depending on the size of the pumpkin, until tender.

2 Meanwhile, make the pastry dough. Put the flour, vegan margarine or butter, and salt into a food processor and blend until it resembles coarse bread crumbs. Alternatively, put the ingredients into a bowl and rub the fat into the flour with your fingertips. Add the water and mix to a dough.

3 Turn out the dough onto a lightly floured surface. Knead briefly, then form into a circle and roll out to fit a 9 inch round tart pan. Trim the edges and reserve the scraps.

4 To make the filling, remove the skin if using fresh butternut squash and chop the flesh. Put the flesh or the pumpkin puree into a food processor with the tofu, brown sugar, molasses, and spices and process to a thick, smooth puree. Pour into the tart shell and gently smooth the surface.

5 Reroll the pastry scraps, brush with soy milk, dredge with a little granulated sugar, and sprinkle with cinnamon. Cut into strips and arrange in a lattice on top of the pumpkin or squash filling. As well as looking attractive, this topping will become crisp, contrasting with the soft filling and helping to hold it together.

6 Bake the pie in a preheated oven, at 350°F, for 40 minutes, until the filling is just set and the topping crisp. Serve hot, warm, or cold, with vegan ice cream or cream or, for vegetarians, thick cream or yogurt.

Dreamy raspberry & rose meringue

This meringue looks sensational yet is easy to make. You can even make it in advance and freeze it in a rigid container. To use, put on a serving dish and let defrost for 1–2 hours before decorating.

SERVES 6

PREPARATION 20 MINUTES

COOKING 1¼ HOURS

4 egg whites

1¼ cups superfine sugar or
    granulated sugar

2 teaspoons cornstarch

1 teaspoon red or white wine vinegar

1 teaspoon vanilla extract

1¼ cups heavy cream

2 teaspoons triple-distilled rosewater

3 cups raspberries

a few red or pink rose petals,
    to decorate

1 Line a large baking sheet with nonstick parchment paper.

2 Put the egg whites into a large, clean, grease-free bowl and whisk until they are thick, glossy, and standing in peaks.

3 Mix together the sugar and cornstarch, then add to the egg whites in 2 or 3 batches, whisking all the time to achieve a beautiful, glossy white meringue mixture. Finally, stir in the wine vinegar and vanilla extract.

4 Spoon the mixture onto the parchment paper, gently spreading it out into a circle 8–9 inches in diameter. Place in a preheated oven, at 350°F, turn the heat down to 300°F, and bake for 1¼ hours, or until crisp. Let cool in the oven if possible.

5 To finish the meringue, whip the cream until it forms soft peaks, then whisk in the rosewater. Pile the cream on top of the meringue, cover with the raspberries, and shower with rose petals. Serve as soon as possible, though it's still fine to eat even after 24 hours.

Jelly & cream sponges

These are like darling little layer cakes. The discarded scraps of cake, jelly, and cream make a great base for a quick trifle, with some fruit, custard, and gelatin.

MAKES 20
PREPARATION 20 MINUTES,
   PLUS COOLING
COOKING 15–20 MINUTES

1 stick butter, softened
⅔ cup granulated sugar
2 eggs
1 cup all-purpose flour
2 teaspoons baking powder
1 tablespoon water
confectioners' sugar, for dusting

FOR THE FILLING

3–4 tablespoons raspberry jelly
   or preserves
⅔ cup heavy cream, whipped

1 Beat together the butter, sugar, eggs, flour, baking powder, and water until light and creamy.

2 Line an 8½ x 12½ inch jellyroll pan with nonstick parchment paper. Spoon the batter into the pan, spreading it to the edges and into the corners. Bake in a preheated oven, at 325°F, for 15–20 minutes, until risen and firm to a light touch. Remove from the pan and let cool on a wire rack.

3 When the cake is completely cold, lay it face down on a board and carefully strip off the backing paper. Cut the cake into 2 equal halves and spread one of them with first the jelly or preserves and then the cream. Press the other half on top, gently but firmly. Using a 1½ inch plain round cutter, cut out 20 circles, then put them onto a plate. (They may look neatest upside down; that way if the sponge on top cracks a little as you cut it, it won't show.)

4 When the cakes are all done, dust with confectioners' sugar and keep them in a cool place until required.

Berry skewers with white chocolate dip

MAKES 20
PREPARATION 15 MINUTES
COOKING 5 MINUTES

1½ cups mixed berries, such as
  strawberries (halved), large
  blueberries, raspberries, blackberries,
  or baby kiwifruit (peeled and halved)

FOR THE WHITE CHOCOLATE DIP

4 oz white chocolate, broken
  into pieces
½ cup heavy cream

1 To make the dip, melt the chocolate in a heatproof bowl set over a
saucepan of gently steaming water. Remove from the heat and stir
in the cream. Put into a small serving bowl and let cool.

2 Put one or two berries on a toothpick—enough for a mouthful—and
continue until all the berries are used. Arrange the berry skewers around
the bowl of white chocolate dip and serve.

Pecan & tarragon-stuffed apricots ⓥ

This is a delicious treat for your vegan party guests, although everyone will enjoy it. You can get vegan cream cheese at good health-food stores and some large supermarkets.

MAKES ABOUT 26
PREPARATION 15 MINUTES,
   PLUS SOAKING

2 cups dried apricots
1¼ cups apple juice
1 cup vegan herb and garlic
   cream cheese
small bunch of tarragon
½ cup pecans

1 Put the apricots into a bowl, cover with the apple juice, and let soak for 8 hours or overnight.

2 Drain the apricots and blot with paper towels. Stuff each apricot with 1 teaspoon of the cream cheese, a small sprig of tarragon, and a pecan. Arrange them, stuffing side up, on a serving plate.

Side dishes

Sesame-roasted asparagus with wasabi vinaigrette ⓥ

If you can make the dressing in advance—24 hours is not too long—the flavor of the wasabi mellows and is delicious and refreshing with the asparagus.

SERVES 4
PREPARATION 10 MINUTES
COOKING 15–20 MINUTES

1 lb asparagus, trimmed
2 tablespoons toasted sesame oil
salt

FOR THE WASABI VINAIGRETTE

2 teaspoons wasabi powder
2 tablespoons warm water
1 tablespoon rice vinegar
1 tablespoon flavorless vegetable oil,
   such as grapeseed
2 tablespoons toasted sesame oil
salt and black pepper

1 Toss the asparagus in the sesame oil, spread out on a baking sheet, and sprinkle with salt. Roast in a preheated oven, at 425°F, for about 15 minutes, or until just tender and lightly browned in places.

2 To make the vinaigrette, put the wasabi into a screw-top jar, add the warm water, and mix to a paste. Add the rice vinegar, vegetable oil, sesame oil, and some salt and black pepper, put the lid on, and shake vigorously for a few seconds until smooth.

3 Arrange the asparagus on individual plates and drizzle the vinaigrette on top. Serve hot, warm, or cold.

Braised whole baby carrots & fennel ⓥ

These vegetables melt in your mouth and their golden liquid supplies a natural sauce for the dish. They are also forgiving; they should be really tender, so it's almost impossible to overcook them, and they can be cooked in advance and gently reheated later if this is most convenient. If there are any leftovers, they also taste good cold.

SERVES 4
PREPARATION 15 MINUTES
COOKING 30 MINUTES

2 bunches of baby carrots
  (about 1½ lb)
12 oz baby fennel
¼ cup olive oil
4 garlic cloves, sliced
1¼ cups water
1 tablespoon lemon juice
salt and black pepper
chopped parsley, to garnish

1 If the carrots are really young, just scrub them; if they're older, peel them. In either case, keep them whole and leave ½ inch or so of the green stems attached at the top. If the fennel is really young and tender, just trim the tops.

2 Put the carrots and fennel into a saucepan with the olive oil, garlic, water, lemon juice, and some salt and black pepper and bring to a boil. Reduce the heat, cover, and cook gently for about 30 minutes, checking occasionally to make sure they're not sticking. They're done when they feel tender to the point of a knife and the water has reduced to a syrupy golden glaze. Sprinkle with chopped parsley and serve.

Parsnips in sage butter

A simple yet wonderful combination of flavors.

SERVES 4
PREPARATION 10 MINUTES
COOKING 15–20 MINUTES

1 lb baby parsnips
2 tablespoons butter, softened
1 tablespoon chopped sage
salt and black pepper

1 Cut the parsnips lengthwise into quarters to create long thin pieces. Put them into a saucepan, cover with water, and bring to a boil, then reduce the heat and simmer for 10–15 minutes, or until tender.

2 Blend the butter with the sage and set aside.

3 Drain the parsnips and put into a warm serving dish, or return them to the saucepan. Season with salt and black pepper, then add the sage butter and serve.

Cabbage with sesame & ginger ⓥ

This simple treatment transforms cabbage. It goes particularly well with Asian-style dishes.

SERVES 4
PREPARATION 5 MINUTES
COOKING 5 MINUTES

1 sweetheart or similar cabbage,
  shredded
1 tablespoon toasted sesame oil
1 tablespoon grated fresh ginger root
1 garlic clove, crushed
salt and black pepper

1 Bring a 1 inch depth of water to a boil in a saucepan, add the cabbage, bring back to a boil, cover, and cook for about 5 minutes, or until the cabbage is tender. Drain.

2 Add the sesame oil, ginger, and garlic to the cabbage and stir well. Season with salt and black pepper and serve immediately.

Roasted potatoes in sea salt & balsamic vinegar ⓥ

Having tried various different oils for roasting potatoes, I've found that canola oil or peanut oil provide the crispiest results.

SERVES 4
PREPARATION 15 MINUTES
COOKING 45 MINUTES

**8 russet potatoes, peeled and
    cut into ½ inch chunks**
canola oil or peanut oil, for roasting
balsamic vinegar
salt and black pepper

1 Put the potatoes into a saucepan, cover with water, and bring to a boil, then reduce the heat and simmer for 7 minutes.

2 Pour ¼ inch of oil into a roasting pan large enough to hold the potatoes in a single layer, then put into a preheated oven, at 400°F, until smoking hot.

3 Drain the potatoes and put them back into the saucepan, then put the lid on the pan and shake to roughen the outsides and make them cook more crisply.

4 Transfer the potatoes to the hot oil and turn them with a large spoon so that the oil covers them all over. Roast for about 35 minutes, or until the potatoes are golden and crisp, turning them over when the undersides are done.

5 Using a slotted spoon, transfer the potatoes to a warm serving dish. Sprinkle generously with salt and black pepper, drizzle with balsamic vinegar, and serve.

Saffron & garlic mashed potatoes

SERVES 4
PREPARATION 15 MINUTES,
   PLUS STEEPING
COOKING 20 MINUTES

9 russet or Yukon gold potatoes
   (about 2¼ lb), peeled and
   cut into even pieces
⅔ cup light cream
good pinch of saffron threads
4 tablespoons butter
4 garlic cloves, crushed
salt and black pepper

FOR THE GARNISH

4 garlic cloves
1 tablespoon olive oil
1 tablespoon chopped parsley

1   Put the potatoes into a saucepan, cover with boiling water, and cook for about 20 minutes, or until tender.

2   Meanwhile, put the cream into a small saucepan with the saffron and bring almost to a boil, then remove from the heat, cover, and let steep.

3   To make the garnish, cut the garlic cloves into thin slices. Heat the olive oil in a small saucepan, add the garlic, and sauté for a minute or so until the garlic is golden. Remove from the heat and set aside.

4   Drain the potatoes, reserving the water, then mash with the butter, crushed garlic, and saffron-steeped cream (no need to remove the saffron threads) to make a smooth, creamy consistency. Add a small quantity of the reserved cooking water, if needed. Season with salt and black pepper.

5   Spoon the potato into a warmed serving dish, top with the fried pieces of garlic, the oil, and some chopped parsley, and serve.

Mashed lima beans & herbs with bok choy ⓥ

SERVES 4
PREPARATION 15 MINUTES
COOKING 10 MINUTES

2 (15 oz) cans lima beans
2 garlic cloves
1–2 tablespoons lemon juice
4 scallions, chopped
2 tablespoons chopped parsley
salt and black pepper

FOR THE BOK CHOY

1 lb bok choy or other Asian
   greens, large pieces halved or
   quartered
1 tablespoon soy sauce
1 tablespoon lemon juice
1 tablespoon toasted sesame oil
1 tablespoon toasted sesame seeds

1 Drain the lima beans, reserving the liquid. Either mash the beans coarsely using a fork or potato masher or, for a smoother mash, blend them in a food processor.

2 Put the mashed beans into a saucepan with the garlic, lemon juice, scallions, parsley, and enough of the reserved bean liquid to make the consistency of mashed potatoes. Season with salt and black pepper. Heat gently and keep warm.

3 Bring a 1 inch depth of water to a boil in a large saucepan. Add the bok choy or other greens, bring back to a boil, cover, and cook for 2–6 minutes, or until it's just tender—the timing will depend on the exact type of greens and the size of the pieces. Drain in a colander, then return to the pan.

4 Add the soy sauce, lemon juice, sesame oil, and sesame seeds to the greens and swirl around to coat them all. Serve with the mashed lima beans and herbs.

Lentils with portobellos, garlic & red wine ⓥ

This is delicious with mashed potatoes or just plenty of lightly cooked cabbage. If you can't find canned lentils, you can use 2 cups cooked green lentils or brown lentils instead.

SERVES 4
PREPARATION 15 MINUTES
COOKING 45 MINUTES

1 tablespoon olive oil
2 onions, chopped
4 garlic cloves, finely chopped
8 portobello mushrooms
2 tomatoes, chopped
a few thyme sprigs
2 bay leaves
1 (15 oz) can green lentils
   or brown lentils
1 cup red wine
2 teaspoons Dijon mustard
salt and black pepper
chopped parsley, to garnish

1 Heat the olive oil in a large saucepan, add the onions, cover, and cook for 5 minutes. Add the garlic, mushrooms, tomatoes, and herbs and stir until lightly coated with the oil. Cover the pan and cook gently for another 10 minutes.

2 Add the lentils with their liquid and the wine, bring to a boil, then cover and let simmer over gentle heat for 30 minutes.

3 Put the mustard into a small bowl, add a little liquid from the pan, and stir to make a smooth cream, then add it to the pan and stir again. Season with salt and black pepper. Garnish with the parsley and serve.

Spicy Thai noodles

SERVES 4
PREPARATION 15 MINUTES
COOKING 20 MINUTES

8 oz rice noodles
2 tablespoons toasted sesame oil
2 teaspoons vegetarian Thai red
   curry paste
6 scallions, finely sliced
walnut-size piece of fresh ginger root,
   peeled and cut into thin shreds
2 garlic cloves, crushed
2–3 tablespoons rice vinegar
1–2 tablespoons shoyu or tamari
2 tablespoons chopped cilantro
salt and black pepper

1 Put the noodles into a bowl, cover with boiling water, and let soak for 5 minutes, until tender, then drain and toss in 1 tablespoon of the sesame oil to prevent the noodles from sticking together. Alternatively, prepare according to the package directions.

2 Meanwhile, heat the rest of the sesame oil in a large saucepan, add the curry paste, and let sizzle for a few seconds. Add the scallions, ginger, and garlic and stir-fry for 1–2 minutes, to cook lightly.

3 Add the noodles to the pan and remove from the heat. Add the rice vinegar, shoyu or tamari, and some salt and black pepper and toss lightly. Stir in the chopped cilantro and serve.

Tandoori paneer

You need a lot of ingredients for this really quick and simple recipe, but it's always popular! You can also make a good vegan version by using firm tofu instead of paneer.

SERVES 4
PREPARATION 10 MINUTES
COOKING 10–15 MINUTES

2 (7½ oz) packages paneer (available in Indian grocery stores), cut into ½ inch cubes
salt
2 tablespoons coarsely chopped cilantro, to garnish
lemon wedges and naan, to serve

FOR THE SPICE MIXTURE

1 tablespoon grated fresh ginger root
1 tablespoon crushed garlic
½ teaspoon hot paprika or chili powder
1 teaspoon turmeric
1 tablespoon ground cumin
2 tablespoons canola oil
2 tablespoons lemon juice

FOR THE SALAD GARNISH

4 tomatoes, sliced
1 small onion, sliced
1 green bell pepper, cored, seeded, and sliced

FOR THE MINT RAITA

1¼ cups plain yogurt (dairy or vegan)
¼ cup chopped mint
salt and black pepper

1 To make the raita, mix the yogurt with the mint and season with salt and black pepper to taste. Put into a serving bowl and set aside.

2 To make the spice mixture, put all the ingredients into a bowl and mix together.

3 Toss the cubes of paneer in the spice mixture and stir to coat them, adding a little salt to taste, remembering that paneer is already salty.

4 Spread the cubes of paneer out on a broiler pan or on a baking sheet that will fit under your broiler and cook under a preheated broiler for 10–15 minutes, turning them a couple of times, until sizzling and crisp.

5 Meanwhile, to make the garnish, mix together the tomatoes, onion, and green bell pepper and put into a serving bowl or onto individual plates. Serve the paneer straight from the broiler, hot and sizzling, with a sprinkling of cilantro on top and lemon wedges. Eat with the salad garnish, warm naan and some mint raita.

Leek rice with almonds & red pepper mayo ⓥ

SERVES 4
PREPARATION 20 MINUTES
COOKING 20–25 MINUTES

1⅓ cups white basmati rice or other
   long-grain rice
1 teaspoon turmeric
2 cups water
5 leeks, cut into 1 inch pieces
2 tablespoons lemon juice
1 tablespoon olive oil
2 teaspoons black mustard seeds
¼ cup toasted slivered almonds
½ cup pitted small green olives
salt and black pepper

FOR THE RED PEPPER MAYO

1 large red bell pepper, halved, cored,
   and seeded
2 tablespoons red wine vinegar
⅓ cup olive oil
2 teaspoons granulated sugar

1 Put the rice into a saucepan with the turmeric and water. Bring to a boil, then reduce the heat as low as possible, cover, and let cook for about 10 minutes, or according to the package directions, until tender. Remove from the heat and let stand, still covered, for 5–10 minutes.

2 Meanwhile, cook the leeks in a saucepan of boiling water for about 10 minutes, or until tender. Drain.

3 Add the lemon juice to the rice along with some salt and black pepper, stirring gently, then mix the leeks into the rice.

4 Heat the olive oil in a small skillet, add the mustard seeds, and heat for 1–2 minutes, or until they're sizzling. Add to the leek mixture, along with the almonds and olives.

5 Meanwhile, to make the mayo, put the red bell pepper halves, cut side down, on a broiler pan and cook under a preheated hot broiler for about 10 minutes, or until black and blistered in places. Cool, then strip off the skin. Blend the bell peppers with the wine vinegar, olive oil, sugar, and some salt and black pepper in a food processor, blender, or using an immersion blender, to make a smooth, thick sauce. Serve with the rice. This dish can be served hot, warm, or cold.

Buckwheat & mango tabbouleh ⓥ

You can buy buckwheat at organic and health-food stores. Be sure to get the raw, untoasted type.

SERVES 4
PREPARATION 10 MINUTES,
   PLUS STANDING
COOKING 3–4 MINUTES

1½ cups raw buckwheat
1 large ripe juicy mango
bunch of mint, chopped
juice of 1 lime
salt and black pepper

1 Put the buckwheat into a dry saucepan and stir over moderate heat for 3–4 minutes, or until the buckwheat smells toasty and is turning light golden brown. Remove from the heat, cover with boiling water, and let stand for 10–15 minutes, until softened.

2 Meanwhile, make 2 cuts through the mango straight down about ¼ inch from each side of the pit. Peel off the skin and cut the flesh into coarse pieces; remove as much flesh from around the pit as you can. Put all the mango flesh into a bowl.

3 When the buckwheat has softened—when you can squash a grain between your finger and thumb—drain it and put into a bowl. Stir in the mango, mint, lime juice, and some salt and black pepper. Eat immediately or store in a cool place for a few hours.

Jamaican jerk sweet potato

It's easy to make your own jerk paste, but for a fast option, use a store-bought one instead.

SERVES 4
PREPARATION 20 MINUTES
COOKING 10 MINUTES

4 sweet potatoes
lime wedges and soft bread, to serve
   (optional)

FOR THE JERK SPICE PASTE

1 onion, coarsely chopped
1 red chile, seeded
4 garlic cloves
4 teaspoons dried thyme
2 teaspoons allspice
1 teaspoon ground cinnamon
½ teaspoon ground nutmeg
2 tablespoons olive oil
1 teaspoon salt
1 teaspoon black pepper

FOR THE CHIVE YOGURT

2 tablespoons chopped chives
1¼ cups plain yogurt
salt and black pepper

1 To make the jerk paste, put all the ingredients into a food processor and process to a paste.

2 Cut the sweet potatoes into wedges about ¼ inch thick—they need to be thin enough to cook through without burning. Spread the cut surfaces of the wedges with the jerk paste and cook under a preheated hot broiler or on a barbecue for 5 minutes on each side, or until the sweet potato is tender to the point of a knife and the jerk paste is crunchy and slightly charred.

3 Stir the chives into the yogurt along with some salt and black pepper, then put into a small serving bowl.

4 Serve the sweet potato wedges immediately while still sizzling hot, accompanied by the chive yogurt, wedges of lime, and plenty of soft bread, if desired.

Quick yeasted herb & garlic flat bread ⓥ

This is an easy bread that you both mix and let rise in the food processor! It couldn't be simpler.

SERVES 4
PREPARATION 20 MINUTES,
   PLUS RISING
COOKING 20–30 MINUTES

3⅔ cups white bread flour
2¼ teaspoons active dry yeast
2 teaspoons sea salt, plus extra
   for sprinkling
1½ cups warm water
⅓ cup olive oil
¼ cup chopped thyme
2 garlic cloves, crushed

1 Put the flour into a food processor fitted with a plastic dough blade. Add the yeast, the 2 teaspoons salt, the water, and 2 tablespoons of the olive oil and pulse until a dough forms, then blend for 1 minute. Let rest, with the lid on, for 45 minutes, or until the dough has doubled in size.

2 Add the thyme and garlic and process briefly to mix, then remove the dough from the machine, divide in half, and press each into a 9 x 5 x 3 inch loaf pan or 8 inch square pan. Cover with plastic wrap and let rest for 1 hour to rise.

3 Press your fingers into the top of the bread a few times and drizzle the rest of the olive oil over the loaves and into the holes, then sprinkle with some sea salt.

4 Bake the loaves in a preheated oven, at 400°F, for 20–30 minutes, or until the loaves are golden brown on top and sound hollow when turned out of the pans and tapped on the bottom. (The timing will depend on the exact size of your pan—the deeper the dough in the pan, the longer it will take to cook.)

5 Cool on a wire rack, or wrap each loaf in a clean dish cloth and let cool slowly if you want the bread to have a soft crust.

Green olives with mixed peppercorns & cilantro ⓥ

Why marinate your own olives when you can buy them? Because they're so easy to make yourself and you can rustle them up when you want them from pantry ingredients—but most of all, because these are divine!

SERVES 4
PREPARATION 10 MINUTES,
   PLUS MARINATING

3½ cups canned large green olives,
   drained
2 garlic cloves, finely sliced
1 lemon
1 tablespoon coriander seeds
1 tablespoon mixed peppercorns,
   such as black, white, green, pink,
   and pimiento
extra virgin olive oil, for marinating

1 Put the olives into a bowl with the garlic. Cut thin strips of zest from half the lemon, using a zester if possible, and add to the olives. Slice the remaining half of the lemon thinly, then cut the slices into smaller pieces again and add to the bowl.

2 Crush the coriander seeds and peppercorns coarsely using a mortar and pestle or by putting them into a strong plastic bag and bashing with a rolling pin. Add to the bowl, then pour in enough olive oil to cover the olives and let marinate for at least 1 hour, or longer if there's time.

Desserts & cakes

White chocolate ice cream with summer berry sauce

SERVES 6

PREPARATION 30 MINUTES,
    PLUS COOLING AND FREEZING

COOKING 10 MINUTES

2 eggs

⅓ cup granulated sugar

1 cup light cream

10 oz white chocolate,
    broken into pieces

1 cup heavy cream

FOR THE SAUCE

8 cups mixed summer berries
    (about 2 lb), such as blueberries,
    raspberries, and blackberries

¼–½ cup granulated sugar

1 To make the ice cream, whisk the eggs and sugar in a bowl. Pour the light cream into a saucepan, bring to a boil, then pour the cream over the eggs. Whisk, then pour the mixture back into the saucepan. Cook over gentle heat, stirring all the time, for a few minutes, until the mixture coats the back of the spoon lightly. Remove from the heat and stir in the white chocolate. Cover and let cool, stirring from time to time to help the chocolate melt.

2 Whip the heavy cream until thick, then fold into the cooled chocolate mixture. Pour into a suitable container for freezing, put into the freezer, and freeze until solid, stirring a couple of times during the freezing process, if possible. Alternatively, freeze in an ice cream maker, following the manufacturer's instructions.

3 To make the sauce, put the fruit and ¼ cup of the sugar into a saucepan and heat gently until the juices run; this will take only a few minutes. Remove from the heat, taste, and add more sugar to taste, if necessary, remembering that the ice cream is sweet, so a sharpness in the sauce makes a pleasant contrast.

4 Remove the ice cream from the freezer about 30 minutes before you want to serve it to let it soften a little, then serve with the sauce.

Little lemon cheesecakes with blueberries

SERVES 6
PREPARATION 25 MINUTES

**25 gingersnaps (about 1½ cups
 when crushed)**
6 tablespoons butter, melted
1¼ cups blueberries
confectioners' sugar, for dusting

FOR THE TOPPING

1⅔ cups low-fat cream cheese
finely grated zest of 2 lemons
2 tablespoons granulated sugar
⅔ cup heavy cream
¼ cup lemon juice

1 Put the cookies into a plastic bag, close the top, then crush with a rolling pin. Put the crushed cookies into a bowl, add the melted butter, and mix to combine. Divide the mixture among six 3½–4 inch round, loose-bottom tart pans, pressing it onto the bottoms in an even layer (don't attempt to go up the sides). Place in the freezer or refrigerator while you make the topping.

2 If there is any liquid on top of the cream cheese, pour it away, then put the cheese into a bowl and add the lemon zest and sugar. Stir to make a creamy mixture, then add the cream and beat until thick. Add the lemon juice and stir with a spoon—the acid in the juice will make the mixture even thicker.

3 Spoon the cream cheese mixture into the tart pans. Spread the mixture to the edges, but don't try to smooth the surface. Chill until required.

4 To finish, lift the little cheesecakes out of the pans—they will come out easily—and gently slide them onto individual plates, removing the bottoms of the pans as you do so. Decorate the tops with blueberries, dust with confectioners' sugar, and serve as soon as possible.

Whiskey cream banana pie

To make the caramel layer you need caramelized condensed milk, which you can make yourself with cans of plain condensed milk. You can caramelize more than one can at a time as long as they are all covered with water as described below. They will keep for months, enabling you to make this dessert quickly. Alternatively, you can buy cans of dulce de leche from some larger supermarkets or online.

SERVES 4–6
PREPARATION 20 MINUTES,
   PLUS COOLING AND CHILLING
COOKING 3–4 HOURS

1 (13–14 oz) can condensed milk or
   dulce de leche (caramel sauce)
36 graham crackers (about 8 oz,
   or 2 cups when crushed)
1 stick butter, melted
2–3 large bananas
1¼ cups heavy cream
¼ cup Baileys cream liqueur
¼ cup grated semisweet chocolate

1   If using condensed milk, put the unopened can into a deep saucepan and add cold water to cover it by at least 2 inches—you can put the pan on its side if it fits better. Bring to a boil, then let simmer for 3–4 hours. Make sure you keep the water level topped so that it's always at least 2 inches above the can (set a timer to remind you). This process is perfectly safe as long as you follow these instructions. Let the can cool in the water.

2   Put the cookies in a large plastic bag, close the top, then crush with a rolling pin to make fine crumbs. Mix the cookie crumbs with the melted butter, then press into the bottom of an 8–9 inch tart pan. If there's time, chill for 10–15 minutes.

3   Peel the bananas and slice each in half lengthwise. Lay the slices of banana, cut side down, in the tart shell, cutting them as necessary to make them fit.

4   Spoon the caramelized condensed milk or dulce de leche evenly over the bananas to cover them.

5   Whip the cream with the Baileys until it forms soft peaks, then spoon on top of the caramel, taking it to the edges of the pie. Sprinkle grated chocolate all over the top. Chill until required—if anything, this tastes even better after 24 hours.

Mango, cardamom & pistachio whips

This is gorgeous, but for a less-rich version, use thick Greek yogurt, or half yogurt and half cream, whipped together.

SERVES 4
PREPARATION 15 MINUTES

½ teaspoon cardamom seeds
1 large ripe mango
1¼ cups heavy cream
2 tablespoons halved, shelled
  pistachios

1 Crush the cardamom seeds using a mortar and pestle, or the end of a rolling pin on a board, removing the outer husks. Set aside.

2 Make 2 cuts through the mango straight down about ¼ inch from each side of the pit. Peel off the skin and cut the flesh into coarse pieces; remove as much flesh from around the pit as you can. Put all the mango flesh into a food processor, along with the cardamom, and process to a puree.

3 Whip the cream until it stands in stiff peaks, then gently fold in the mango puree, not too thoroughly, to create a pretty marbled effect. Spoon the mixture into 4 glasses and top with the pistachios.

Microwave-steamed maple syrup cake

Once in a while, it's nice to have a real indulgence and it's also fun to do some "real" cooking in the microwave. I like to make this on a dreary winter's day, perhaps for Sunday lunch. It's so quick, you can do it on the spur of the moment.

SERVES 4

PREPARATION 20 MINUTES,
  PLUS STANDING

COOKING 10 MINUTES

1½ sticks butter, softened, plus extra
  for greasing
¾ cup granulated sugar
⅓ cup milk or milk and water
1⅓ cups all-purpose flour
1 tablespoon baking powder
3 eggs
⅓ cup maple syrup, plus
  extra to serve (optional)
toasted chopped walnuts, to decorate

1 Put the butter, sugar, milk, flour, baking powder, eggs, and 1 tablespoon of the maple syrup into a food processor and process to a creamy consistency. Alternatively, put the ingredients into a bowl and beat with a wooden spoon or wire whisk until light and fluffy.

2 Pour the remaining maple syrup into the bottom of a lightly greased, plastic 1¼-quart microwave-proof bowl, then spoon the cake batter over the syrup.

3 Microwave, uncovered, until the cake has risen and a toothpick inserted into the center comes out clean. This takes about 10 minutes, depending on the power of your microwave. You can cook it for a few minutes, then have a look and see how it's getting on—it won't ruin it.

4 Let the cake stand for a few minutes, then turn out onto a warmed serving plate (or you could serve it straight from the bowl, if you prefer), so that the golden syrupy top is uppermost, and decorate with the walnuts. Serve with extra maple syrup, if desired.

No microwave?
If you don't have a microwave, you can steam the cake batter, but omit the milk or water. Make a pleat in a piece of aluminum foil, place it over the top and sides of the bowl, and tie with string around the rim of the bowl—or, much easier, use a plastic bowl with a snap-on lid. Put the bowl into a steamer fitted over a saucepan of boiling water and steam for 1½ hours, checking the level of the water from time to time and topping off with boiling water, if necessary.

Cappuccino meringues

Meringues are a wonderful fat-free treat and easy to make; the filling can be as indulgent or virtuous as you desire.

MAKES 12 HALVES
PREPARATION 15 MINUTES
COOKING 2 HOURS

2 egg whites
1 teaspoon good-quality instant coffee granules
⅔ cup superfine sugar or granulated sugar

FOR THE FILLING

⅔ cup fromage blanc, low-fat crème fraîche, or Greek yogurt
cocoa mix, for dusting

1 Line a baking sheet with nonstick parchment paper.

2 Put the egg whites and instant coffee granules into a large, clean, grease-free bowl and whisk until thick—the peaks formed must be able to hold their shape and you should be able to turn the bowl upside down without the mixture coming out. However, don't get it to the point where the whisked eggs start to break up and lose their volume. Add the sugar a tablespoon at a time, whisking after each addition.

3 Put tablespoons of the mixture onto the parchment paper, leaving a little space between them. Bake in a preheated oven, at 250°F, for 2 hours, until they have dried out. If possible, turn off the heat and let them stand in the oven until completely cold.

4 To finish the meringues, sandwich pairs together with a good spoonful of your chosen filling, put on a plate, and dust with a little cocoa mix. Eat within about 2 hours.

Vanilla-poached figs ⓥ

A great way to turn less-than-perfect figs into a succulent treat. The vanilla beans can be used again. Remove them after use, rinse under running water, and let dry. A good way to store them is buried in a jar of granulated sugar; this absorbs their flavor and keeps them dry—and makes vanilla sugar.

SERVES 4
PREPARATION 10 MINUTES
COOKING 30 MINUTES

2 cups water
3 tablespoons granulated sugar
2 vanilla beans
8 fresh figs
1 cup plain Greek yogurt,
   to serve (optional)

1 Make a light syrup by putting the water, sugar, and vanilla beans into a saucepan large enough to hold the figs, bring to a boil, and simmer for 5 minutes.

2 Add the figs to the pan. Bring to a boil, then cover and cook over gentle heat for 20 minutes, or until the figs are plump and tender when pierced with the point of a sharp knife.

3 Remove the figs from the pan with a slotted spoon. In each fig, make a cut lengthwise, almost to the bottom of the fruit, then another cut perpendicular to it. Place in a shallow serving dish. Boil the syrup and vanilla beans hard for a few minutes, until it has reduced a little and thickened. Pour the syrup over the figs. Serve hot, warm, or cold, with the yogurt, if desired.

Chili kulfi

SERVES 4

PREPARATION 15 MINUTES,
   PLUS STANDING, COOLING,
   AND FREEZING

COOKING 5 MINUTES

3 cups light cream

¼ teaspoon dried red pepper flakes

10 cardamom pods, crushed

a good pinch of saffron threads
   (optional)

¾ cup granulated sugar

2 teaspoons rosewater

¼ cup ground almonds (almond meal)

3 tablespoons chopped pistachio nuts

a few fresh rose petals or extra
   pistachios, to decorate

1 Put the cream into a saucepan with the red pepper flakes, cardamom pods, and saffron, if using. Bring to a boil, then remove from the heat, cover, and let stand for 10–15 minutes for the flavors to steep.

2 Strain the mixture into a bowl and add the sugar, stirring until it dissolves. Stir in the rosewater, ground almonds, and pistachio nuts and let cool.

3 Line four ⅔ cup individual dessert molds, ramekins, or disposable cups with plastic wrap, then pour in the cooled kulfi mixture, dividing it evenly among them, and freeze until solid.

4 Remove the kulfi from the freezer about 15 minutes before you want to serve them. Turn them out of the containers onto dishes, peel off the plastic wrap, and serve, sprinkled with a few fresh rose petals, if available, or extra pistachios.

Espresso risotto

Whenever possible, I prefer to use soy milk instead of cow milk. Soy milk is healthy for us and it adds a creamy flavor to this risotto as well as to sauces. This risotto is also good cold, with the whipped cream folded in.

SERVES 4
PREPARATION 10 MINUTES,
   PLUS STANDING
COOKING 35–40 MINUTES

⅔ cup risotto rice
⅔ cup water
1 tablespoon good-quality strong
   instant coffee granules
2½ cups soy milk
2 tablespoons unsalted butter
2 tablespoons rum
⅔ cup heavy cream, lightly whipped
1–2 tablespoons coffee sugar crystals,
   to decorate (optional)

1 Put the rice and water into a medium saucepan, bring to a boil, and simmer for 5 minutes.

2 Add the coffee granules and soy milk. Bring to a boil, then let boil gently, stirring often, for 20–30 minutes, or according to the package directions, until the rice is tender and the mixture is thick.

3 Remove from the heat, add the butter and rum, cover, and let stand for 10 minutes, or until ready to serve.

4 Serve into warmed individual bowls, each topped with a generous spoonful of whipped cream and a sprinkling of coffee sugar granules, if desired—or pass around the cream and the sugar separately.

Honey & ginger pashka
with bitter chocolate sauce

SERVES 4
PREPARATION 10 MINUTES,
    PLUS OVERNIGHT CHILLING
COOKING 5 MINUTES

4 tablespoons unsalted butter, softened

¼ cup thick honey

2 cups ricotta cheese

grated zest of 1 orange and 1 lemon

½ teaspoon vanilla extract

¼ cup chopped candied orange or
    lemon peel

2 pieces of drained and chopped
    preserved ginger in syrup

½ cup toasted slivered almonds

a few edible fresh flowers, to decorate
    (optional)

FOR THE SAUCE

4 oz bittersweet chocolate,
    broken into pieces

⅓ cup water

1 Line the inside of a clean plastic flowerpot, measuring 6 inches across the top, with pieces of parchment paper.

2 Put the butter into a food processor or large bowl with 2 tablespoons of the honey, the ricotta, citrus zests, and vanilla extract and blend together, then stir in the candied peel, ginger, and half the almonds.

3 Spoon the mixture into the flowerpot and level the surface. Stand the flowerpot in a bowl—to catch the liquid that will leak out—and let stand in the refrigerator for 12–24 hours.

4 Just before you want to serve the pashka, make the sauce by melting together the chocolate and the water in a small saucepan over gentle heat.

5 To serve, invert the flowerpot over a plate; the pashka will slide out easily and you can then peel off the paper. Quickly heat the remaining honey in a small saucepan and pour over the top of the pashka to make a glaze, which will run down the sides. Top with the remaining almonds and decorate around the base with a few fresh flowers, if you desire. Serve with the chocolate sauce in a small pitcher or bowl.

Coconut & honey ice cream with banana-sesame fritters

SERVES 4

PREPARATION 10 MINUTES,
   PLUS FREEZING

COOKING 35 MINUTES

1¾ cups coconut milk
3 tablespoons thick honey
1⅓ cups heavy cream
lime wedges, to serve

FOR THE BANANA FRITTERS

1 cup all-purpose flour
1 teaspoon baking powder
2 teaspoons granulated sugar
¾ cup water
canola oil, for deep- or pan-frying
2 large bananas, cut into
   ½ inch diagonal slices
3 tablespoons sesame seeds

1 First make the ice cream. Put the coconut milk into a bowl and whisk to remove lumps, then whisk in the honey and cream. Pour into a suitable container for freezing, put into the freezer, and freeze until firm, whisking it a couple of times during the freezing process. Alternatively, freeze in an ice cream maker, following the manufacturer's instructions.

2 Remove the ice cream from the freezer 30 minutes or so before you want to serve it to let it soften a little.

3 To make the fritters, put the flour, baking powder, and sugar into a bowl and gradually stir in the water to make a coating batter.

4 Heat the canola oil in a deep fryer or deep, heavy saucepan until a few drops of the batter when added to the pan sizzle and rise immediately to the surface of the oil. Dip slices of banana in the batter, then slide into the hot oil—don't add too many at a time. Cook until the batter is crisp and golden brown, then remove the fritters with a slotted spoon, drain on paper towels, and sprinkle with the sesame seeds.

5 Continue until all the fritters are done, then serve immediately, with wedges of lime and scoops of the coconut ice cream.

Honeydew melon, strawberry & mint compote ⓥ

You can't tell by its scent whether a honeydew melon is ripe, so buy from a reputable supplier at the end of summer to be sure of one with succulent, sweet, and melting flesh.

SERVES 4
PREPARATION 15 MINUTES,
   PLUS STANDING

½ cup mint leaves
⅓ cup granulated sugar or honey
1 ripe honeydew melon
1 lb strawberries, hulled and sliced
   (about 3 cups)

1 Put the mint leaves into a large bowl and crush lightly with the end of a rolling pin or a wooden spoon. Add the sugar or honey and crush the leaves again by pressing them against the side of the bowl with a wooden spoon. Set aside.

2 Halve the melon, then scoop out and discard the seeds. Scoop out the flesh with a melon baller, or simply use a sharp knife to cut the flesh away from the skin and into bite-size pieces.

3 Put the melon into a bowl with the mint and add the strawberries. Stir, then cover and let stand for 1–4 hours for the flavors to blend. The fruit compote will produce its own liquid and is deliciously refreshing served cold, but not icy.

Spicy vegan carrot cake ⓥ

SERVES 4
PREPARATION 20 MINUTES
COOKING 1¼ HOURS

2¼ cups shredded carrots
1 cup raisins
⅓ cup canola oil or olive oil
⅔ cup unrefined granulated sugar
2 cups all-purpose flour
2 teaspoons baking powder
1 teaspoon grated nutmeg
1 teaspoon ground cinnamon
½ cup apple juice concentrate
   (available from health-food stores)
   or maple syrup
¼ cup orange juice

FOR THE FROSTING

1 cup dairy-free alternative
   to cream cheese
grated zest of 1 orange
2 tablespoons granulated sugar
strands of orange zest, to decorate

1 Line an 8 inch square cake pan with nonstick parchment paper.

2 Put the carrots, raisins, canola oil or olive oil, and unrefined granulated sugar into a bowl and mix. Add the flour, baking powder, nutmeg, cinnamon, apple juice, and orange juice and mix again until everything is combined—the batter will be sticky.

3 Spoon the batter into the prepared cake pan and level the surface. Bake in a preheated oven, at 325°F, for 1¼ hours, or until a toothpick inserted into the center comes out clean. Let stand in the pan until completely cold.

4 To make the frosting, mix the dairy-free alternative to cream cheese with the orange zest and granulated sugar, then spread over the top of the cold cake. Decorate with strands of orange zest.

Grilled pineapple with jaggery & crème fraîche

The pineapple can be cooked under a hot broiler, but the very nicest way to do it is on a barbecue at the end of the main cooking, when the embers are dying down—it makes a wonderful end to an alfresco meal.

SERVES 4
PREPARATION 10 MINUTES
COOKING 10 MINUTES

1 large ripe juicy pineapple
neutral-tasting oil, such as canola oil
   or light olive oil, for brushing
¾ cup jaggery, chopped
   if in a solid block
1¼ cups crème fraîche or plain
   Greek yogurt, to serve

1 Cut the pineapple lengthwise through the leaves, first in half, then into sixths or eighths, depending on the size of the pineapple; it's best if the wedges are no more than about ½ inch thick. Brush them all over with the cooking oil.

2 Put the pineapple slices on a broiler pan and cook under a preheated broiler, or cook on a barbecue grid. Cook for about 10 minutes in all, turning them halfway through cooking when the first side is tender and, if on a grid, attractively marked by it. Remove from the heat and sprinkle with some of the jaggery.

3 Serve the pineapple with bowls of the crème fraîche or Greek yogurt and jaggery for people to help themselves.

Melting chocolate cakes

Little melting chocolate cakes have become a modern classic—and these provide a new twist because when you cut them open, white chocolate oozes out! They are easy to do and can be prepared well in advance, ready for cooking just before serving.

SERVES 4
PREPARATION 25 MINUTES
COOKING 20 MINUTES

4 tablespoons butter, plus extra
    for greasing
4 oz semisweet chocolate, broken
    into pieces
2 eggs
¼ cup granulated sugar
½ teaspoon vanilla extract
1 tablespoon all-purpose white flour
8 squares good-quality white chocolate
unsweetened cocoa powder, for dusting
thick cream, to serve

1 Line the bottoms of four ⅔ cup individual metal dessert molds or ramekins with circles of nonstick parchment paper, then butter them thoroughly.

2 Melt the semisweet chocolate and butter in a heatproof bowl set over a saucepan of gently steaming water. Stir, remove from the heat, and let cool slightly.

3 Using an electric mixer, beat together the eggs, sugar, and vanilla extract until thick and pale; this takes at least 5 minutes.

4 Gently fold the melted chocolate and flour into the beaten mixture until completely incorporated. Put 1 tablespoon of the chocolate batter into each dessert mold and place in a preheated oven, at 400°F, for 5 minutes, then remove them and quickly fill the molds with the rest of the batter. Drop 2 squares of the white chocolate into each. Put them back into the oven and bake for 11–12 minutes, or until risen and a little crusty around the edges.

5 Remove from the oven and let stand for 1–2 minutes. Slip a knife around the sides of the molds, then invert each cake over a warmed plate. Let stand for another 30 seconds, and gently lift off the mold. Dust the cakes with a little cocoa powder and serve immediately with thick cream.

Little plum upside-down cakes with cinnamon custard

Metal baking rings are ideal for making these, but if you don't have any, you could use shallow 4 inch loose-bottom tart pans lined with circles of nonstick parchment paper.

SERVES 4
PREPARATION 30 MINUTES
COOKING 30 MINUTES

butter, for greasing
⅔ cup granulated sugar, plus extra
   to taste
8 plums (about 1 lb), pitted and sliced
¼ cup water

FOR THE CAKES

2 eggs
¼ cup granulated sugar
⅓ cup all-purpose flour
¼ teaspoon baking powder

FOR THE CUSTARD

2 egg yolks
1 teaspoon cornstarch
1 tablespoon granulated sugar
1¼ cups whole milk
½ cinnamon stick

1 Line a baking sheet with nonstick parchment paper, grease generously with butter, and place four 4 inch metal baking rings on it. Sprinkle inside the rings lightly with some of the sugar.

2 Put the plums into a saucepan with the rest of the sugar and the water. Cover and cook over moderate heat for 3–4 minutes, or until the plums are just tender but not collapsed. Remove from the heat. Taste and add more sugar, if necessary.

3 To make the cakes, beat the eggs and sugar together until thick and pale; this takes about 5 minutes with an electric mixer. Sift the flour and baking powder over the top and fold in gently with a spatula.

4 Divide the plums among the rings, spreading them out so that they cover the whole area. Spoon the cake batter on top, leveling it off. Bake in a preheated oven, at 350°F, for 20 minutes, or until the cakes spring back when touched lightly in the center.

5 To make the custard, put the egg yolks, cornstarch, and sugar into a bowl and beat together. Pour the milk into a saucepan, add the cinnamon stick, and bring to a boil. Gradually whisk the hot milk into the egg mixture, then return the mixture to the pan and stir over gentle heat for a few minutes, until the mixture thickens and coats the back of a spoon. Remove the cinnamon stick. The custard can be served hot or cold.

6 Run a knife around the edges of the rings, then turn out each cake onto a warmed serving plate and serve with the custard separately.

Pear & brioche charlotte

SERVES 4
PREPARATION 25 MINUTES,
  PLUS COOLING
COOKING 1¼ HOURS

4 pears, peeled, cored, and
  cut into pieces
2 tablespoons granulated sugar
2 tablespoons water
1 vanilla bean
8–10 slices of brioche
1 stick butter, melted
1 cup mascarpone cheese
2 egg yolks
2 tablespoons demerara sugar
  or other raw sugar
thick cream, to serve (optional)

1 Put the pears into a saucepan with the granulated sugar, water, and vanilla bean. Bring to a boil, then reduce the heat, cover, and let cook gently for about 30 minutes, or until the pears are tender. Let stand until completely cold.

2 Brush the slices of brioche with the melted butter and arrange them in an 8 inch round springform cake pan, or a shallow ovenproof casserole, covering the bottom and sides and saving some slices for the top.

3 Beat the mascarpone a little to soften. Mix in the egg yolks and the pears together with any liquid. Spoon the mixture on top of the brioche, then put the remaining brioche slices on top, brush with the melted butter, and sprinkle with the demerara sugar.

4 Bake in a preheated oven, at 350°F, for about 40 minutes, or until the charlotte is golden, crisp, and set in the middle; cover it with a piece of aluminum foil toward the end of the cooking time if it seems to be getting too crisp on top before the inside is set.

5 Serve hot, warm, or cold, with cream, if you desire.

Banana & Earl Grey cake

The bergamot oil, which you can get at any health-food store or online, intensifies the flavor of the Earl Grey in this stylish cake.

SERVES 4
PREPARATION 10 MINUTES,
   PLUS STANDING
COOKING 30–35 MINUTES

8 Earl Grey tea bags
1 cup boiling water
1 large banana
1 stick butter, softened
⅔ cup firmly packed brown sugar
2 eggs
1⅔ cups all-purpose flour
3½ teaspoons baking powder

FOR THE ICING

1⅓ cups confectioners' sugar
1 teaspoon butter
1 drop of bergamot essential oil
   (optional)

1 Add the tea bags to the boiling water in a heatproof bowl, making sure they're all submerged. Cover with a plate and let stand until cold.

2 Squeeze the tea bags to get as much liquid from them as possible, then discard the tea bags and measure out ⅔ cup of tea. Put the measured tea into a food processor or mixer (reserve the rest). Peel and mash the banana and add to the tea in the food processor with the butter, brown sugar, eggs, flour, and baking powder, then blend or beat until the batter is light and fluffy.

3 Line a 7–8 inch cake pan with nonstick parchment paper. Spoon the batter into the pan and gently level the surface. Bake in a preheated oven, at 350°F, for 30–35 minutes, or until a toothpick inserted into the center comes out clean. Cool for a minute or so in the pan, then turn out onto a wire rack and let stand until cold.

4 To make the icing, put the confectioners' sugar into a saucepan with the butter, bergamot oil, if using, and 2 tablespoons of the remaining tea. Stir over the heat until the butter has melted. Pour over the top of the cake and let set.

Lemon & almond drizzle cake with berries

SERVES 4
PREPARATION 25 MINUTES,
  PLUS STANDING
COOKING 40–45 MINUTES

1½ sticks butter, softened
¾ cup plus 2 tablespoons
  granulated sugar
2 eggs
finely grated zest of 1 lemon
1⅓ cups all-purpose flour
½ cup ground almonds (almond meal)
1 tablespoon baking powder
crème fraîche or Greek yogurt, to serve

FOR THE DRIZZLE TOPPING

¼ cup lemon juice
1¼ cups confectioners' sugar

FOR THE BERRIES

4 cups mixed berries, such
  as raspberries, strawberries,
  blueberries, or red currants
  (any stems and hulls removed,
  halved or quartered if large)
granulated sugar, to taste

1 Line a 9 x 5 x 3 inch loaf pan with a strip of nonstick parchment paper to cover the bottom and narrow sides.

2 Put the butter, granulated sugar, eggs, lemon zest, flour, ground almonds, and baking powder into a bowl and beat together until creamy.

3 Spoon the batter into the prepared loaf pan and gently level the surface. Bake in a preheated oven, at 325°F, for 40–45 minutes, until risen and firm to a light touch and a toothpick inserted into the center comes out clean.

4 Five minutes before the cake is done, make the drizzle topping. Mix the lemon juice and confectioners' sugar in a small saucepan, then stir over gentle heat until the confectioners' sugar has dissolved.

5 As soon as the cake comes out of the oven, prick the top all over and pour the confectioners' sugar mixture over the top. Let cool, then remove the cake from the pan and strip off the paper.

6 Prepare the fruit an hour or so before you want to eat. Put it into a bowl, sprinkle with granulated sugar to taste, and let stand for 1 hour, stirring from time to time. Taste and add a little more sugar, if necessary. Serve the fruit and cake with a bowl of crème fraîche or Greek yogurt.

Fig tarte tatin with ginger cream

This is also delicious made with apricots. Make exactly as described, using 5 cups of halved, pitted apricots instead of the figs.

SERVES 4
PREPARATION 25 MINUTES
COOKING 30 MINUTES

12 oz frozen ready-to-bake all-butter
   puff pastry (see page 295)
3 tablespoons butter
18 figs (about 1¾ lb), halved
¼ cup granulated sugar
¼ cup toasted slivered almonds
   (optional)

FOR THE GINGER CREAM

1 cup heavy cream
3 pieces of preserved ginger,
   finely chopped

1   Roll the pastry a little on a floured surface to make it a little thinner if you can, then cut a circle to fit ½ inch larger than the top of an 8 inch tart pan or cake pan.

2   Melt the butter in a skillet. Add the figs, cut side down, and the sugar. Cook over high heat for about 6 minutes, until the figs are slightly browned and caramelized.

3   Put the figs, cut side down, into the tart pan or cake pan and scrape in all the gooey juice from the saucepan.

4   Put the pastry on top, tucking it down into the figs at the sides. Prick the pastry, then bake in a preheated oven, at 400°F, for 20–25 minutes, until crisp and golden brown.

5   Meanwhile, make the ginger cream. Whip the cream until it forms soft peaks, then fold in the ginger. Transfer the cream to a bowl and chill until required.

6   To serve, loosen the tart with a knife, then invert over a plate. The figs will be on top. Sprinkle with the almonds, if using, then let settle for a couple of minutes before serving with the ginger cream.

Individual meringues with pomegranate & grenadine

SERVES 4
PREPARATION 15 MINUTES,
  PLUS STANDING
COOKING 40 MINUTES

2 egg whites
⅔ cup superfine sugar or
  granulated sugar
1 teaspoon cornstarch
¼ teaspoon vinegar

FOR THE FILLING

2 ripe pomegranates
¼ cup grenadine
1¼ cups heavy cream, whipped

1 Line a large baking sheet with nonstick parchment paper.

2 Put the egg whites into a large, clean, grease-free bowl and whisk until they are thick, glossy, and standing in peaks. Add the sugar a tablespoon at a time, whisking after each addition, then fold in the cornstarch and vinegar.

3 Spoon the mixture onto the parchment paper, making 4 saucer-size circles, and hollow each out in the center a little. Bake in a preheated oven, at 275°F, for about 40 minutes, or until crisp on the outside but still soft within. Cool on the baking sheet. If possible, turn off the heat and let stand in the oven until completely cold.

4 While the meringues are cooking, cut the pomegranate in half and bend back the skin—as if you were turning it inside out—to make the seeds pop out. Put the pomegranate seeds into a small bowl with the grenadine and let steep.

5 To finish the meringues, spoon some whipped cream onto each, then top with the pomegranate seeds and their juice. Serve as soon as possible.

Fruit sushi plate ⓥ

A plate of sweet sushi rice and lemon grass-scented fruits makes a pretty and refreshing dessert.

SERVES 4
PREPARATION 20 MINUTES,
    PLUS COOLING
COOKING 25 MINUTES

FOR THE RICE

1 cup glutinous rice, risotto rice, or
    other short-grain rice
¼ cup granulated sugar
1¾ cups coconut milk
1 vanilla bean
juice of 1 lime

FOR THE FRUIT

⅔ cup granulated sugar
½ cup water
1 lemon grass stalk, crushed
½ teaspoon dried red pepper flakes
juice and pared zest of 1 lime
1 star fruit (carambola), thinly sliced
1 large ripe papaya, peeled, seeded,
    and sliced
2 kiwifruits, peeled and sliced

1 Put the rice and sugar into a saucepan with the coconut milk and vanilla bean. Bring to a boil, then reduce the heat, cover, and let cook gently for 20 minutes, or according to the package directions, until the rice is tender and the liquid has been absorbed. Remove from the heat, gently stir in the lime juice, and let cool.

2 Meanwhile, make an aromatic syrup for the fruit. Put the sugar and water in a saucepan with the lemon grass, red pepper flakes, and lime zest. Heat gently until the sugar has dissolved, then bring to a boil and remove from the heat.

3 Put the star fruit in a single layer on a plate and pour the hot syrup over it, together with the lemon grass and lime zest. Cover and let stand until cold, then remove the lemon grass and lime zest, squeeze them to extract all the flavor, and discard them. Sprinkle with the lime juice.

4 To serve, form the sweet sushi rice into small circles ¾ inch in diameter and ½ inch thick and arrange on plates. Top with the star fruit, papaya, and kiwifruit slices and spoon the syrup over them. Serve the remaining fruit on the side.

Nectarines roasted with lavender ⓥ

The wonderful taste of summer on a plate—and so easy to do.

SERVES 4
PREPARATION 10 MINUTES
COOKING 25 MINUTES

3 tablespoons butter
3 tablespoons demerara sugar
  or other raw sugar
2–3 dried heads of lavender
6 nectarines, halved and pitted
chilled Greek yogurt, to serve

1 Select a shallow casserole that will hold all the nectarine halves in a single layer, grease generously with half the butter, and sprinkle with half the sugar and half the lavender.

2 Place the nectarine halves, cut side down, in the buttered casserole, dot with the rest of the butter, and sprinkle with the remaining sugar and lavender.

3 Bake, uncovered, in a preheated oven, at 350°F, for about 25 minutes, or until the nectarines are tender. Serve hot or warm, with some chilled Greek yogurt.

Orange creams with caramel sauce

This is a great mixture of flavors and textures. The orange creams can be topped with crisp, shiny golden caramel if you have a cook's blowtorch, or you can place them under the broiler—either way, they're delectable.

SERVES 4
PREPARATION 30 MINUTES,
   PLUS COOLING AND CHILLING
COOKING 45 MINUTES

FOR THE ORANGE CREAMS

1¼ cups heavy cream
2 pieces of pared orange zest
6 egg yolks
⅓ cup granulated sugar

FOR THE ORANGES

4 ripe sweet juicy oranges
granulated sugar, to taste

FOR THE CARAMEL SAUCE

4 tablespoons butter
⅓ cup heavy cream
¼ cup firmly packed brown sugar

1 Line the bottoms of 4 ramekins with circles of parchment paper.

2 To make the orange creams, put the cream and orange zest into a saucepan and bring to a boil. Remove from the heat and let cool slightly. Remove the orange zest.

3 Whisk together the egg yolks and 2 tablespoons of the granulated sugar to blend, then gradually whisk in the cream. Pour the mixture into the prepared ramekins, stand them in a roasting pan, and pour in boiling water to come halfway to three-quarters of the way up the sides of the ramekins. Bake in a preheated oven, at 275°F, for about 30 minutes, or until the custards are just firm in the centers. Remove from the oven, cool, then chill.

4 Cut the skin and pith from the oranges, then cut the segments out of the white inner skin. Put the segments into a bowl with a little granulated sugar to taste, if necessary, and chill until required.

5 For the sauce, put the butter, cream, and brown sugar into a saucepan and heat gently for 2–3 minutes to make a golden caramel sauce.

6 To serve, loosen the sides of the orange creams and turn out onto plates, then remove the lining paper. Top each with a thin layer of the remaining granulated sugar and heat with a cook's blowtorch to make a hard, glazed golden topping. Alternatively, turn them out onto a heatproof plate that will fit under your broiler, top each with a thin layer of sugar, and broil for 1–2 minutes to make the caramel, then carefully transfer each to a serving plate. Arrange some orange slices on each plate and drizzle some caramel sauce around the oranges. Serve immediately.

Pink Champagne granita marbled with raspberries ⓥ

This recipe makes the most wonderful ending to a special meal. You probably won't need all the granita—it might be called for as second helpings and it makes a wonderful pick-me-up for the cook (or anyone else!) the morning after, perhaps with some freshly squeezed pink grapefruit juice added. Incidentally, ordinary Champagne, rather than pink, is also great to use, but not as pretty.

SERVES 4

PREPARATION 15 MINUTES,
    PLUS COOLING AND FREEZING

COOKING 5 MINUTES

1 cup water
1¼ cups granulated sugar
1 bottle pink Champagne
3 cups raspberries

1   Put the water into a saucepan with 1 cup plus 2 tablespoons of the sugar. Heat gently until the sugar has dissolved, then bring to a boil and remove from the heat. Let cool.

2   Mix the cooled sugar syrup with the Champagne. Pour into a shallow container so that the mixture is about ½ inch deep and put into the freezer, stirring the mixture from time to time as it becomes frozen around the edges. Because of the alcohol in the Champagne, it will take up to 4 hours to freeze and will never become rock hard, so it can be used straight from the freezer. It's fine to make it the day before needed.

3   To serve, first toss the raspberries in the remaining sugar and set aside for a few minutes, until the sugar has dissolved. Put the raspberries into 4 serving glasses. Give the granita a quick stir with a fork, then scrape some into the glasses on top of the raspberries and serve immediately.

Affogato with almond tuiles

This is an easy-to-make yet wonderful ice cream. Although freshly brewed espresso is the perfect topping for this—whisper it quietly—instant espresso is also fine. By the time it has mixed with the ice cream, I defy anyone to tell the difference!

SERVES 4
PREPARATION 30 MINUTES,
   PLUS FREEZING
COOKING 15–20 MINUTES

2½ cups heavy cream
1 (13–14 oz) can condensed milk
⅔ cup strong espresso coffee

FOR THE ALMOND TUILES

1 egg white
¼ cup granulated sugar
3 tablespoons all-purpose white
   flour, sifted
2 tablespoons butter, melted
⅓ cup slivered almonds
flavorless vegetable oil, such as
   grapeseed, for greasing

1   To make the ice cream, beat the cream until it forms soft peaks. Add the condensed milk to the cream and beat again until combined. Transfer to a suitable container for freezing and freeze until firm.

2   To make the tuiles, line a large baking sheet with nonstick parchment paper. Whisk the egg white until stiff, then beat in the sugar. Add the flour and butter alternately to make a smooth mixture. Place big teaspoons of the batter well apart on the parchment paper (you'll probably get about 4 to a large sheet) and, using the back of the spoon, spread the batter out to make circles each about 4 inches in diameter. Sprinkle the top of each with the almonds, then bake in a preheated oven, at 350°F, for 4–5 minutes, until set and lightly browned, especially around the edges.

3   Remove from the oven and let cool for a minute or so until firm enough to lift from the baking sheet. Meanwhile, oil a rolling pin. Drape the tuiles over the rolling pin so that as they cool they become curved. Once they're cool, they can be removed to a wire rack.

4   Continue with the rest of the batter to make about 16 tuiles. When they're all cold, store in a container until required.

5   To serve, scoop the ice cream into 4 bowls. Pour a couple of tablespoons of the hot coffee over each and serve immediately, with the tuiles.

White chocolate gelato with citrus drizzle

Because of its light consistency—made mainly with milk instead of cream—gelato takes longer to freeze than normal ice cream and, for this reason, I find it best to use the freezer instead of an ice cream maker. Having said that, this gelato couldn't be simpler to make.

SERVES 4
PREPARATION 15 MINUTES,
    PLUS COOLING AND FREEZING
COOKING 15 MINUTES

3 cups milk
10 oz white chocolate, broken
    into pieces
1½ teaspoons cornstarch
½ cup heavy cream

FOR THE CITRUS DRIZZLE
juice and finely grated zest of 1 orange
juice and finely grated zest of 1 lime
½ cup granulated sugar

1 To make the ice cream, put the milk into a saucepan and bring to a boil. Remove from the heat and stir in the chocolate.

2 Put the cornstarch in a small bowl with some of the cream and blend to a smooth paste. Reheat the chocolate milk, then pour it into the cornstarch mixture, stir, and return it to the saucepan, along with the rest of the cream. Bring to a boil, stir for a minute or so until it thickens, then remove from the heat and let cool.

3 Pour the cooled mixture into a suitable container for freezing, put into the freezer, and freeze until solid, stirring from time to time during the freezing process, if possible.

4 To make the citrus drizzle, put the orange and lime juices and zests into a small saucepan with the sugar and gently bring to a boil. Reduce the heat and simmer for about 5 minutes, until reduced in quantity and slightly thickened (watch carefully because it burns easily). Set aside until required.

5 To serve, remove the ice cream from the freezer about 30 minutes before you want to serve it to soften a little, then scoop into bowls. Check the citrus drizzle; if it has become too thick, lighten it a little by stirring in a teaspoon or so of hot water. Then swirl some citrus drizzle over the top of each portion and serve immediately.

Chocolate truffles

These heavenly truffles have rich, creamy centers like Belgian chocolates and are absolutely worth the effort.

MAKES ABOUT 22
PREPARATION 30 MINUTES,
   PLUS CHILLING
COOKING 5 MINUTES

FOR THE WHITE CHOCOLATE
AND COFFEE TRUFFLES

4 oz white chocolate, broken
   into pieces
2 tablespoons cold unsalted butter,
   cut into small pieces
⅓ cup cold heavy cream
½ teaspoon instant espresso coffee
1 teaspoon boiling water
4 oz melted white chocolate, sifted
   unsweetened cocoa powder, or finely
   ground toasted hazelnuts, to coat

FOR THE MILK CHOCOLATE
TRUFFLES WITH SOFT CENTERS

4 oz milk chocolate, broken
   into pieces
2 tablespoons cold unsalted butter,
   cut into small pieces
2 tablespoons cold heavy cream
1 teaspoon brandy (optional)
4 oz melted milk chocolate, sifted
   unsweetened cocoa powder, or finely
   ground toasted hazelnuts, to coat

1 To make the white chocolate and coffee truffles, melt the white chocolate in a heatproof bowl set over a saucepan of gently steaming water. Take the bowl off the heat and stir in first the butter and then the cream. Dissolve the coffee in the boiling water and stir into the mixture, then chill in the refrigerator for about 1 hour, until firm.

2 Divide the white chocolate mixture into 10 even pieces and form into balls. Place these on nonstick parchment paper and put into the freezer to chill thoroughly for about 1 hour.

3 To coat with chocolate, dip the frozen chocolates into the melted white chocolate—it will set quickly—coating both sides. Alternatively, roll the truffles in cocoa powder or finely ground toasted hazelnuts. Put them on nonstick parchment paper and chill in the refrigerator until required.

4 To make the milk chocolate truffles, melt the milk chocolate in a heatproof bowl as before, then remove from the heat and beat in the butter, cream, and brandy, if using. Chill in the refrigerator until fairly firm, then proceed as described for the white truffles, using milk chocolate, cocoa powder, or nuts to coat.

5 Store all the truffles in the refrigerator until required.

Notes on ingredients

Agar powder A vegetarian substitute for gelatin available from supermarkets; use in the same way as gelatin powder.

Almond butter Available with no added ingredients such as emulsifiers, from good health-food stores. There is a brown version and a white one. The oil may separate in the jar—just give it a good stir before use.

Arame seaweed A delicately flavored seaweed, available dried from good health-food stores, as are other seaweed varieties. Simply wash and soak briefly before use.

Bergamot oil An essential oil, a small quantity of which can be used as a flavoring; available from health-food stores.

Buckwheat Strictly speaking, a seed, although usually classified as a grain. Available from organic food stores, raw or toasted. I prefer to buy raw and, if required, toast it briefly in a dry saucepan before use.

Chickpea, or besan, flour A type of flour made from chickpeas. Available in large supermarkets and Indian and Middle Eastern stores.

Coconut milk Organic coconut milk is much nicer than the nonorganic type (which has unnecessary additives) and there's no point in buying the low-fat version as it's just coconut milk with water added—you might as well buy the whole type and add your own water.

Curry leaves Can be found in some large supermarkets and Asian or Indian food stores. They freeze well, so buy a good supply of fresh ones when you see them—just put them into the freezer and use when required.

Daikon A large tapered white radish with a slightly hot flavor, available from supermarkets and Asian stores. Turnip can be substituted.

Eggs Use free-range, preferably organic, eggs.

Epazote A herb with a pungent, savory flavor, often used in Mexican bean recipes to make the beans less gas-inducing. Dried epazote can be found in Mexican stores. The herb savory, which is said to have the same effect, can be substituted, or mixed herbs can be used for flavor.

Garam masala A mixture of ground spices added toward the end of cooking to enhance the flavor. Every enthusiastic Indian cook has their own recipe, made from spices that they roast, mix, and grind themselves, but a store-bought mixture is fine.

Hoisin sauce A thick, brown, sweet, and savory sauce available from supermarkets and Chinese stores.

Jaggery, or palm sugar A brown unrefined sugar used throughout Asia. It is available from large supermarkets and is often sold as a solid block. Dark brown sugar can be substituted.

Kaffir lime leaves Can be bought dried, in a jar, from some large supermarkets or from Asian food stores; use them quickly before they lose their magical fragrance.

Ketjap manis A type of soy sauce from Indonesia, which is sweeter and less salty than most other types. It can be found in some large supermarkets or Asian food stores. Alternatively, you can sweeten ordinary soy sauce with some honey. Store indefinitely in a cool, dry place.

Kombu Dried seaweed used for the preparation of Japanese stock. Available in Asian stores and health-food stores.

Kuzu (Japanese starch) Available in Japanese and health- food stores. Arrowroot or cornstarch can be used instead.

Lemon grass Long, tapering grasslike stalks with a lemon flavor. Crush and cook in the recipe, then remove before serving, or remove the tough outer skin and use just the tender center part, sliced.

Masa harina A type of cornmeal used to make tortillas. You can buy it at Mexican food stores and in large supermarkets.

Mirin A sweet fortified yellow Japanese wine used only for cooking. Found in Asian stores and some large supermarkets.

Miso Fermented soy paste. Generally speaking, the lighter the miso, the milder the flavor and greater the sweetness. Available in health-food stores and Asian stores. To get the full health benefits, buy unpasteurized miso and do not boil or overheat it in order to retain its health-giving enzymes.

Nori Seaweed, sold in flat sheets, for use in sushi rolls. Buy pretoasted nori from Asian and health-food stores.

Nutritional yeast Dried "inactive" yeast in the form of flakes, available in a container from upmarket health-food stores. It has a pleasant cheesy, nutty taste—and is rich in many nutrients.

Pastry From a health and flavor point of view, I prefer pure butter pastry. You can get several types of pastry in the frozen food sections in the supermarkets. Let puff pastry thaw for 30 minutes, phyllo for 24 hours—or look in Greek or Middle Eastern food stores for fresh phyllo.

Porcini mushrooms in white truffle paste Both truffle oil and porcini and white truffle paste can be found in large supermarkets or Italian food stores.

Ras el hanout A Moroccan spice mixture that you can buy at Middle Eastern food stores.

Rice vinegar A light, delicate vinegar made from rice wine. Available in large supermarkets and Asian stores. Wine vinegar (red or white) can be substituted, but use a little less.

Sake A pale golden Japanese wine made from rice, with 15–17 percent alcohol. Available in Asian stores. White wine or dry sherry can be substituted.

Sesame oil Dark sesame oil can be found in any supermarket and it gives a unique and delectable flavor to Asian dishes. You need only a small amount.

Shiitake mushrooms Chinese mushrooms, available fresh from many supermarkets and Asian stores.

Soy flour A type of flour made from soybeans. Available in some supermarkets and health-food stores.

Sugar I like to use unbleached Fair Trade organic sugar. It is not much different in flavor compared to the refined white stuff, but is grown without the use of pesticides and similar chemicals. Because it is Fair Trade, the farmers receive a fair price for their crops.

Tahini Like peanut butter, but made from sesame seeds, without additives. I prefer the pale version, which is easy to find in supermarkets and health-food stores.

Tamari, shoyu, and soy sauce Shoyu is the Japanese word for soy sauce. It is an all-purpose flavoring enhancer; tamari is wheat-free with a stronger flavor. It's important to make sure you buy brands that are traditionally brewed, natural, and organic. Available from some big supermarkets and from health-food stores.

Tamarind A long brown pod with seeds and a tangy pulp used throughout Asia as a souring ingredient. Tamarind paste can be found in jars in Indian food stores. Lemon juice can be used instead.

Tempeh A naturally fermented soybean product, like tofu, but made from whole soybeans instead of soy milk. Pale tempeh is usually the best to start with because it has the mildest flavor. Available in health-food stores.

Teriyaki sauce A sweet sauce made from equal parts of soy sauce and mirin (or soy sauce, sake, and sugar to taste). It is available in supermarkets and Asian stores, or you can mix your own.

Thai curry paste Most contain shrimp or other fish paste, but search for vegetarian red and green curry paste available on some online sites or in health-food stores.

Tofu Tofu is found in the chilled food section of most supermarkets. The type most widely available is "firm." I've mostly used this in the recipes because it's a reliable all-purpose type of tofu, suitable for slicing and frying or, with liquid added, for making into a dip or dressing. You can buy other fine, delicate types of tofu in Asian food and organic stores and these are delicious and worth experimenting with if you like tofu.

Toor dhal This is a small golden lentil. It has an earthy, almost smoky flavor and makes a beautiful dhal. Sometimes it's coated in oil to preserve it—wash this off by rinsing it in hot water before cooking. Yellow split peas would be the best substitute.

Umeboshi plums/umeboshi paste These have a delicious salty sharpness that enhances many foods. Refrigerated, they will last for ages in their jar. Buy from good health-food stores.

Unsweetened soy cream Containers of soy cream equivalent to light cream can be found in health-food stores and supermarkets in the UK. It does contain a little sugar, but not enough to make it "sweet"—check the label. In the United States it is not so easy to find; substitute unsweetened soy milk, which has a creamy consistency when cooked.

Vegetable stock Marigold vegetable bouillon, a powder which comes in a tub, makes beautiful vegetable stock. Most supermarkets sell it, as do health-food stores, and there is also a vegan version that doesn't contain lactose.

Vegetarian Worcestershire sauce Can be bought from health-food stores. (The problem with ordinary Worcestershire sauce is that it contains anchovy extract.)

Vinegars While you can get away with just one type of vinegar—I'd choose organic cider vinegar—it's useful to have two or three different ones. Rice vinegar is light and suitable for Chinese and Japanese dishes, while balsamic has a wonderfully rich, sweet flavor: the more you spend on it, the better it will be.

Wakame seaweed A leafy seaweed, a little like spinach to look at and with a mild, yummy flavor of the sea. Available dried from good health-food stores.

Wasabi A strong green Japanese horseradish condiment with a hot mustard taste. It is available as a powder or a paste in Asian food stores. English mustard can be substituted.

Wild mushrooms Supermarket wild mushroom mixtures can be good value, although for a real treat and a no-expense-spared meal, nothing can replace a few precious chanterelles, morels, or some fresh porcini. Although they're expensive, because they weigh little, you get a lot for your money. Dried mushrooms are good value—I especially like dried morels that you can buy at some big supermarkets.

Notes on the recipes

Frying

The healthiest way to deep-fry is to use canola oil or peanut oil, which are stable at high temperatures (and therefore healthier), and discard them after use. I use a wok, which has a large surface area so you use less oil or, if I'm doing just a little frying, a small saucepan. For shallow pan-frying and roasting I generally use olive oil, which is my standard all-purpose oil, but please refer to the individual recipe.

To broil and skin a red bell pepper

To broil and skin a red bell pepper, cut the bell pepper in half and remove the core, stem, and seeds. Place the halves, rounded side up, on a broiler pan and broil on high for about 10 minutes, or until the skin is blistered and black in places and the flesh tender. Remove from the heat and let cool, then peel off the skin.

Toasting hazelnuts

If you're starting with the skinned type (which are the most widely available), either toast them under a hot broiler for a few minutes, stirring them after 1–2 minutes so they toast evenly, or put them on a baking sheet and roast in a moderate oven, at 350°F. They'll take only 8–10 minutes, so watch them carefully and remove them from the hot baking sheet immediately when they're done so they don't go on browning. To toast unskinned hazelnuts, that is, those still in their brown skins, proceed as described, but they'll take about 20 minutes in the oven. Let them cool, then rub off the brown skins with your fingers or a soft cloth.

Alcoholic drinks

Some wines and alcoholic drinks are prepared using animal by-products, such as gelatin, although increasingly many are vegetarian or vegan. Read the label or check with the supplier to be sure.

Unfamiliar ingredients

Many ingredients from other countries, as well as vegetarian and vegan products, are now available online, so if you are struggling to find some of the ingredients in this book in local supermarkets, try searching for them on the Internet.

Making recipes vegan

Many of the recipes in this book are naturally vegan and are labeled as such. A lot more can easily be made vegan by making simple substitutions, such as using olive oil or vegan margarine instead of butter, soy instead of dairy cream, maple syrup instead of honey, and vegan puff pastry (read the label) instead of all-butter puff pastry. Here are some suggested vegan alternatives:

Suggested vegan alternatives

NONVEGAN	VEGAN
butter	vegan margarine
milk	soy milk
cream	soy cream
yogurt	soy yogurt
cream cheese	vegan cream cheese
goat cheese	vegan cream cheese
feta cheese	vegan feta cheese
cheddar	vegan cheddar
(or other firm) cheese	(or other firm) cheese
Parmesan-style cheese (grated)	vegan Parmesan cheese
paneer	firm tofu or firm vegan cheese
mayonnaise	vegan mayonnaise
hollandaise sauce	vegan mayonnaise
honey	maple syrup

Index

Author acknowledgments

Many talented people have been involved with the production of this book and I'd like to acknowledge them all. In particular, Eleanor Maxfield, commissioning editor, who had the initial idea and masterminded this book; Clare Churly, my editor, for her hard work; Jo Murray, who did such an excellent job on the proofs; Will Webb, for the beautiful new design; and also Jonathan Christie, Jennifer Veall, and Katherine Hockley. It was so satisfying to see this book take shape from my two previous books—*Vegetarian Supercook* and *Veggie Chic*—and I'm thrilled with the result. I would also like to thank Sarah Ford, who commissioned those two books and worked closely with me, and the people who helped to produce them: Alison Goff, Sue Bobbermein, Tracy Killick, Jo MacGregor, Rachel Lawrence, Jessica Cowie, Barbara Dixon, Jo Lethaby, Ian Paton, Martin Crowshaw, Rachel Jukes, Liz Hippisley; and the wonderful photographers and food stylists, Gus Filgate and David Martin, who worked their genius for *Vegetarian Supercook*, and Jason Lowe and Sunil Vijayakar, who did the same for *Veggie Chic*. I'd also like to say a special "thank you" to Ant Jones of CliQQ Photography and *Cook Vegetarian Magazine* for my photo; to my daughter Claire for her help with creating and testing recipes for *Veggie Chic*; to my agent Barbara Levy for all her help and advice; and to my dear husband Robert for mammoth dish-washing sessions and so much besides: Thank you all from my heart.

Picture acknowledgments

Octopus Publishing Group/Gus Filgate and Jason Lowe
Author portrait: Ant Jones/CliQQ Photography (www.cliqq.co.uk)

An Hachette UK Company
www.hachette.co.uk

First published in Great Britain in 2013 by
Hamlyn, a division of Octopus Publishing Group Ltd
Endeavour House
189 Shaftesbury Avenue
London
WC2H 8JY
www.octopusbooksusa.com

This edition published in 2014

Copyright © Octopus Publishing Group Ltd 2013
Text copyright © Rose Elliot 2013

Distributed in the US by
Hachette Book Group USA
237 Park Avenue
New York NY 10017 USA

Distributed in Canada by
Canadian Manda Group
165 Dufferin Street
Toronto, Ontario, Canada M6K 3H6

This material was previously published in *Vegetarian Supercook* (2004) and *Veggie Chic* (2006).

ISBN 978-0-600-62877-4

Printed and bound in China

10 9 8 7 6 5 4 3 2 1

Commissioning Editor: Eleanor Maxfield
Managing Editor: Clare Churly
Art Director: Jonathan Christie
Design by Will Webb
Picture Library Manager: Jennifer Veall
Assistant Production Manager: Caroline Alberti